FATHERING
WORDS

ALSO BY E. ETHELBERT MILLER

Andromeda
The Land of Smiles and the Land of No Smiles
Migrant Worker
Season of Hunger/Cry of Rain
Where Are the Love Poems for Dictators?
First Light
Whispers, Secrets and Promises

EDITOR

Synergy: An Anthology of Washington D.C. Black Poetry
Women Surviving Massacres and Men
In Search of Color Everywhere

FATHERING WORDS

The Making of an African American Writer

E. ETHELBERT MILLER

St. Martin's Press
New York

Often the father is more than abser
he is lost, as he has been lost to hir
elf for most of his adult lif
rushed by his burdens, render
mpotent by fears and anxietie
integer, in the army or the factory
the marketplace. The son goes
earch of the father, to be reconcil
in a healing embrace. In that act
ove he restores his father's lost pri
nd manhood. Perhaps he also fin
imself.

THOMAS DUNNE BOOKS.
An imprint of St. Martin's Press.

FATHERING WORDS: THE MAKING OF AN AFRICAN AMERICAN WRITER.

www.stmartins.com

Thanks to the Henry Dumas Estate for permission to use the poem
"Image," which appears in *Play Ebony Play Ivory* and *Knees of a Natural
Man*. Copyright © 1968–1999 by Loretta Dumas and
Eugene B. Redmond.

Design by Heidi J. H. Eriksen

Library of Congress Cataloging-in-Publication Data
Miller, E. Ethelbert.
    Fathering words : the making of an African American writer /
E. Ethelbert Miller.—1st ed.
        p.   cm.
    ISBN 0-312-24136-4
    1. Miller, E. Ethelbert. 2. Miller, E. Ethelbert—Family. 3. Afro-
American poets—Biography. 4. Poets, American—20th century—
Biography. 5. Fathers and sons—United States. 6. Afro-American
families. I. Title.
PS3563.I3768 Z465 2000
811'.54—dc21
[B]   00-024293

First Edition: June 2000

10   9   8   7   6   5   4   3   2   1

THIS BOOK IS DEDICATED TO THE FOUR WOMEN
WHO HELPED WITH THE MOTHERING OF *Fathering Words:*

Denise King-Miller
Jenny Bent
Meri Danquah
Don Mee Choi

ACKNOWLEDGMENTS

Special thanks to St. Martin's Press for believing in this book. I will always be grateful to my editors Melissa Jacobs and Kristen Nardullo.

Often the father is more than absent; he is lost, as he has been lost to himself for most of his adult life, crushed by his burdens, rendered impotent by fatigue and anxieties, reduced to a number, a statistical integer, in the army or the factory of the marketplace. The son goes in search of the father, to be reconciled in a healing embrace. In that act of love he restores his father's lost pride and manhood. Perhaps he also finds himself.

–*Stanley Kunitz*

Life can only be understood backwards, but it must be lived forwards.

—*Søren Kierkegaard*

FATHERING WORDS

CHAPTER ONE

I

The day after my brother died, Carmen, one of his neighbors, said she saw him walking his dog. My brother Richard, who had changed his name to Francis, loved animals and so he took the name of the saint he loved.

Growing up in the South Bronx it was important to believe in something, and so my brother made the decision to believe in God. I met God one afternoon on Longwood Avenue in the Bronx. It must have been around 1958 and I was attending P.S.39, which was located near streets like Beck, Kelly, and Fox. Longwood Avenue was the "big street" and I was not permitted to cross it alone. I was in one of those grades in school where you took naps and the teachers gave you cookies when you were good. On the day I met God I had been standing on the corner for almost an hour afraid to cross Longwood Avenue. All my school friends were gone and I was alone with cars passing by and the dark evening creeping in like one of my sister's boyhood lovers. I was afraid to cross the street without holding someone's hand, and so I did something my brother was good at doing. I started praying to God. I asked God to come for me, to help me cross the big street. If he did, I promised I would be good for the rest of my life. I would never steal or lie. I closed my eyes and only opened them when I heard my father running across the street, cursing and trying to fix his clothes at the same time. When I was little I thought my father was God.

Sitting in the back of a black limousine, parked on a hill in a cemetery near Yonkers, on a cold day in December 1985, I saw my father cry for the first time in my life. It was one of those moments when the world slows down and you notice the color of air. You stare at your hands and wonder how long you will live or which member of the family you will bury next. My father, Egberto Miller, dressed in black, his shoes polished in a way he could never teach my brother or me, sat in the limousine waiting to return home from Richard's funeral. I watched him raise his hands and heard him mumble one word, "gone." Maybe this is how God will end the world. He will say one word and end everything. No fire or rain. I listened to my father, repeating one word and knew he would never be comforted again. Little did I know that another black limousine would come for me in two years. It would take me to my father's funeral. On that day I would begin to search for my own words in order to make sense out of my loss. All the men in my family were suddenly—gone.

In the past whenever I was troubled I could sit down and write a few poems. But what I am recovering from now is a different type of heart surgery. Sorrow and grief can be found in that place within the blues where words end and moans begin. The singer is speechless because the hurt is so bad. The only thing one can do is ride the song.

A few years ago, I remember reading the second chapter of Doctorow's *Billy Bathgate* in which Billy explains how it was juggling that got him to where he was. This is how it feels to be a writer. I need to write about my father

2

and brother. The story, however, is too deep and heavy for poems. I need to father more words and explain the beginning. Maybe it starts with a young boy coming to this country from Panama, a place where the oceans kiss. Or maybe the threads of this story begin with a man on his knees in a monastery, praying to his mother instead of God. I would like to believe this story can be told while I am juggling.

Several members of my family described me as a "blue baby" when I was born. Richard was born with six fingers. So both of us were the subject of early family stories. One of my cousins claimed I was supposed to be given to her mother to be raised. Only Richard's crying prevented this. When I returned from the hospital I became the baby of the family. My sister was happy with this new development.

There were many things that took place before my birth. My family owned pets such as roosters. My father had not yet found employment in the post office. He was a coffee-colored man with two children to feed and clothe. He met my mother dancing at the Savoy. The war was going on in Europe and the dreams of black people could be seen hanging from fire escapes. Neighborhoods were changing. Folks were leaving Harlem for the Bronx. It was like moving to the suburbs. Egberto Miller would find the 1940s a challenge as he listened to the new sounds of bebop coming from the jazz clubs.

Egberto, who was called Eddie by his friends, became a young man with only a few coins in his pocket. He had been a baby in the arms of a woman too young and too fast to slow down. In the old country, a canal had been built. West Indians came from every island to find work. A frontier of water separated them from "paper gold." Malaria, accidents, broken promises were enough for some to

3

lose hope and others to believe in their own destiny. America was like heaven, far off to the north. It was the place where a great uncle would plant and harvest the first seeds of success. Investing in real estate, he would later send for other members of his family. His mother would bring his sisters and brothers to America. One child already had a child, she was my grandmother Marie. It was her mother who decided we would all be Millers, and so the ties to Panama were cut. Egberto's father became a ghost. His own family geography disappeared because of a woman's desire and need to forget. Many years later a writer would be born into the family searching for stories to tell. There would be a decision made to take him back to the hospital or perhaps even give him away.

II

*W*hen they brought the baby home I was so excited. I pushed Richard out of the way. I remember holding Eugene for the first time. He was smaller then some of my dolls. I thought he would break. My mother thought I was silly. My name is Marie. I was named after my grandmother. I was the bald-headed child. My father often refused to take me out in the stroller if my head was not covered. He could not believe a girl could be born without any hair. I must have been five or six before my mother could hold something in her hands and make a braid. The reason I had no hair is because I was yet to be trusted with the family stories. I was not wise enough to understand why people acted the way they did, especially men. My mother would have to teach me these things, along with cooking, cleaning, and dressing myself. My hair would grow with each story I learned to remember. Now that I am over fifty years old, my hair is long and beautiful. There are places where it has turned gray, and here I find myself wanting to forget my memory.

My brother Eugene wants me to tell him what happened before he was born. He is a writer now and maybe he will realize how much is missing or has become what he calls whispers and secrets. I have always been trusted because I was a girl they wanted to become a woman. I belong to a family of mostly women. Everyone it seems is an aunt and lives in Brooklyn. They are women who hold onto their West Indian accents like spices and the silver bangles that dance around their arms. I believed their power could be found in their jewelry or how they sat in chairs on Sunday afternoons, their wide hips and large arms taking up the space of rooms. One could listen all day to kitchen conversations. Words mixing with the smell of food. Once I learned how to cook I knew I would be accepted into this magical club of women. My mother, the oldest of three sisters, would instruct me how to cook not from books but from watching. One could only learn if one was quiet and watched. There was never any time for questions. So, what I know about my family is what I know. It is difficult to explain or make sense out of some of the things that happened. I don't understand all the pain and guilt that has accumulated over the years. I can't explain why my father was filled with so much rage and so much love. I wonder why my mother seldom closed her eyes except for a few minutes each day. She was a woman who heard and knew the source of every sound inside and outside her apartment. As children, we could not escape her watch. Our mother saw everything. When I told her Carmen saw Richard walking his dog after he died, she said that was foolish devil talk. I don't believe everything my mother tells me anymore. I think she saw Richard after he died, I think she was talking with him in the kitchen one morning while making my father breakfast.

III

My father had no father. Instead he had an English name on a Spanish birth certificate. It was a document he could not read. He kept it among medical and financial records. A birth certificate mixed up with old receipts, health and bank statements, contained in a metal box, the kind you associate with burglaries and semiprecious jewels. Whenever one of my parents opened the "tin" they did so in the back of the apartment, with shades and curtains closed. It would be many years later, after college, a first marriage, a few published books that I would be permitted in the same room with the metal box. How shocked and disappointed I was to discover that much of what the box held was junk. There were things my parents held onto because they felt the papers were important. Documents with small print and legal jargon. Both my parents were baffled by words. I knew my father was unable to read much of what he had collected. But what could he hide? His father did not suddenly walk out a door, turn a corner, and disappear. He never came to America. In the movie the boat moves slowly from the dock, the passengers look back at the land, lovers, and the past.

Farewells are different from good-byes. The separation more permanent. The farewell can be romantic, like a tear falling from an eye. A woman leaving behind a relationship no stronger than the tide. The good-bye could have been blessed by a parent angry at a daughter's early pregnancy. Seldom during his life did my father escort anyone to the front door to shake their hands, pat them on their backs, and wish them well.

No father, what does that mean? Is it just a theme in books, articles in newspapers, and conference topics? I have found it to be an ingredient in numerous conversations. Black boys need black fathers.

It is the 1930s and Egberto is learning the streets of Harlem like so many others. He will have many addresses and receive little schooling, the movement from place to place imitating the improvisation of a jazz solo. A few years before his death my father sent me out shopping for an entire day looking for a Miles Davis composition. What was the name of that song? Or the one he asked my mother to dance to when he met her at the Savoy.

A family struggles to find its own rhythms, the duets between brothers and sisters, husbands and wives, mothers and daughters, fathers and sons. The family music escapes through open windows and closed doors. It can be upstairs, downstairs, or next door. The music is the joy of weddings and birthdays, the slow sadness of illness and funerals. It is the overcrowded housing projects and the empty playgrounds too dangerous for play. The music is what raises us and teaches us to sing. Sometimes it makes you want to dance, and you need a partner. You must learn to play the beat, setting the tone and tempo, hoping someone will hear your lament and leap in and pull you out of depression. Family music, and Egberto hears the space in between notes. The place where a father's smile and hand should be.

IV

The green Dodge begins to move backward slowly down the hill. My mother and I are in the front seat. My father went into the store to purchase ice. The car is rolling backward. Behind us a man is looking under the hood of his own vehicle. His legs will soon be trapped between the two cars. There is nothing my mother and I can do. She has never learned how to drive and cannot operate the brakes. The man's screams come through the back window of our car. My father comes rushing out of the store. He panics before running to the car. On this day I lose all desire to learn how to drive. I will join a long list of writers who cannot drive and become as different as the music of Sun Ra.

My father's Dodge is the car that took us to the beach. I don't remember going anywhere else. Why was my father so attracted to water? He could not swim. In the summer on his days off from work we would pack food and blankets and go to Jones Beach. Some times we went to Far Rockaway and had to be reminded of how once someone had stolen my father's clothes at the beach and he had to ride the subway home in only his bathing suit. Incidents like this make you want to buy ice. How else can one keep the soda cold and the sandwiches fresh? On the day before we went to the beach my father would polish his car and get it ready for the journey. I guess the Dodge was like a boat. The kind his father refused to board or was not invited to place his foot on. A car with enough room for five. After the green Dodge would come a black one. By this time my brother would be getting ready to enter the monastery. The fun of going to the beach would end. The ice would melt.

V

I hated the beach because the sand would get in my hair. Eugene would make those silly castles with a red pail and yellow shovel. He also walked along the shore looking for seashells. Our father would be far out in the water, unable to swim but capable of jumping up and down and making his own waves. Strange how near the water my father would become so happy and warm. Maybe he was baptizing himself, beginning to believe in his own power. There were times when we were the only black people at the beach and our skins would glow and wink back at the sun.

VI

I let the water cover my ankles. Behind me my mother and father are sitting on a blanket. I will forget this day along with many others. My childhood, like my first marriage, is almost gone from my memories. What tide claimed them before old age? Why is it so difficult to remember those days in New York? I want to see my father's face again. I want him to talk this time. I cannot watch him sleep throughout eternity. I must wake him from his dreams. When I was standing on a corner of Longwood Avenue and my father came to get me, it was like someone crossing a huge ocean or walking on water. I opened my eyes and my father was there.

For much of my life I tried to connect with him. When I would come home in the early seventies from college, I attempted to talk with him more than my mother. My father was usually in the bedroom with the television playing.

"Hi, Gene," he would say as I kissed him. It was often a glance across his beard. My father was not a fan of kissing and hugging. Our conversations were always brief and I would leave my father alone in his bedroom with a pillow behind him and I would walk back into the kitchen to talk to my mother.

How did it feel to lie in bed and listen to laughter coming from the kitchen? My father was an outsider even within his own family. Nothing much had changed from when he was a boy living in Harlem. He would come back to his grandmother's house and the food that was set aside for him to eat would be gone. It was the thirties and the grayness of the period would cover black people like ash. Food and clothing would disappear like work. Apartments were overcrowded and families struggled to make ends meet.

I knew my parents were not wealthy. I knew my mother and father were not poor. Still, in the fifties, there were days without heat and hot water and one was encouraged to take care of one's shoes. My mother believed that you could tell a man by his shoes. During the good times we could buy Buster Browns. It was important to keep your shoes polished and the heels in good condition.

As the black limousine slowly moved down the hill in the cemetery, I sat in the back seat with my sister, Marie. I looked at my shoes. The sun was shining on this cold February day. My father had been cremated and perhaps we should have taken his ashes to the beach. We could have rented a boat and sailed to the center of some isolated spot. Marie and I could have held hands. We could have made a wish or said a prayer. We could have scattered our father's ashes across the water with the knowledge that he never learned to swim but loved the waves. We could say good-bye to our father, our eyes looking back at the shore.

CHAPTER TWO

I

When I was ten I wanted to live inside my father's dreams. My father worked nights and slept during the day. Our apartment on 938 Longwood Avenue in the fifties was what someone coming from the South, or maybe Texas, might call a shotgun shack. My family lived in unit number three. One walked up several stairs from the front stoop past the mailboxes, a long corridor, and then up a long flight of stairs. The first door on the right was where we lived. Inside, the rooms were next to each other like shoe boxes. Off the hallway, was a bedroom, bathroom, kitchen, then a living room, with two more bedrooms in the back. A fire escape outside the bedroom on the left. During the years I would grow up in this space, the rooms would change. Bedrooms would become living rooms. A kitchen would become a bathroom if there was no hot water. Richard's room would become Marie's room. I saw my father sleeping in many different rooms.

A man sleeps because he is tired. He also has a thirst for sleep if he wishes to escape. Maybe after drinking or making love, the wetness of sleep can wash away a man's pain or guilt. A man can also crave sleep if he wishes to dream. Here a man can discover his wings. He can learn to fly again. He can leave this world for another. To dream is to be free. For my father to dream it was the chance to slip past the labels and the gravity of opinions that people had of him. He could avoid being called dumb or stupid. He could fix anything you gave him. I remember a large picture of my father that was stored in the back of a closet. In the picture my father is handsome, cool, debonair, a lady's man, Billy Dee Williams when Diana Ross was Lady Day. My father was in his twenties when this picture was made. He had the look of a gambler, or maybe Malcolm Little before he took an X for his name.

We lived on Longwood Avenue because some cousin or uncle helped my father find a place to live. Here was a man with three children, trying to make ends meet. He needed all the help he could get. On those late afternoons when he would leave the house for work he would ignore the sky and clouds. He would have no time to name the trees, plants, or flowers. My father walked down the street the way jazz musicians entered clubs carrying their instruments. He had a presence of coolness, detachment. A musician turning his back to his audience.

Egberto Miller walks to the subway carrying his lunch. My mother has taken the time to fix him a good meal. I will remember the exchange of small brown paper bags more then hugs and kisses between my parents. When we moved into the St. Mary's Housing Projects, we lived on the seventeenth floor; my mother would watch my father walk to work from the bedroom window. Behind her would be an unmade bed. The outline of my father's body was still trapped against the sheets and blankets. My father never overslept when it was time to go to work. He never dragged himself out of bed. He was up and in the bathroom washing his body before you could

12

even talk to him. This is why I believe he never dreamed. His eyes never had that soft, hazy, distant look. His eyes never looked tired. When you work hard everyday you don't look tired; you are tired but you never mention it. There are no excuses.

I wonder what my mother thought about my father always sleeping. No time to really go anywhere. What was she thinking while bending over the stove? My father is sitting at the kitchen table. He props his head up with his hands. He is waiting for his meal. Years from now I will recognize this pose. It's the picture we get from the losers' locker room after the World Series, the Super Bowl or the NBA Finals. It's defeat after making an error, the ball going in and out of the rim. A foot touching the line in the end zone. Or worst, the referee or umpire missing the call. Yet there is something heroic about my father. It took many years for me to realize the simple beauty behind how he ate his food. The care that he gave to even the most mundane task.

Just before I went off to college, he printed my name on the inside of a new typewriter case, his block letters so beautifully even. I looked at my name each time I took the typewriter out. I was named by the women in the family. A great aunt gave me the middle name Ethelbert. My mother's mother was named Eugen without the E at the end. I write my name on a white sheet of paper, Eugene E. Miller. I hand it to my father so he can spell it correctly.

II

I liked to watch my father draw. He could make faces and animals. My daddy also liked to take pictures with his camera, so I would wear a pretty dress like it was Easter Sunday. I would hold Richard's hand and pretend he was my husband. How funny we were. Pictures are only good when you're a star. I wanted to be in movies. It was a childhood dream. When I attended Morris High School, I was very popular. I ran for student government and passed out M&M candy. Vote for Marie Miller, M&M, for vice president.

III

My father could have left my mother when I was young. He stayed perhaps because no one expected him to stay. When the music is over, some men escort their women back to their seats or the wall they were standing against. They have no intention of walking them home. When my father met my mother, she was still living in Brooklyn with her father and two sisters, Winnie and Evelyn. I can imagine my father taking the subway to see the woman he was falling in love with.

Egberto counts the station stops. He is wearing his good clothes. As the train races into darkness he closes his eyes. For a brief moment he dreams. The softness of my mother's flesh, the sweetness of her hair wraps around his fingers. Egberto believes he has found what he has been looking for all his life. Suddenly, in his dream, a tall man appears and grabs his hands. He pulls Egberto off the train.

If you were from Harlem it was better to stay away from the Brooklyn girls. Some guys would pull a blade and leave you with a scar. A border, a boundary, a gang claiming its place. Nothing changes. If you are walking in the wrong neighborhood then you must be wrong. No explanation or excuses. You better run and not get caught. New clothes or old, someone can cut you and make you bleed. My father knew the risks and he measured the weight of love in his heart. Love is like an anchor holding its own. When the train comes to my father's stop, he exits and looks both ways.

The only person who will give my father trouble is my grandfather. Edgerton Marshall ran a tight ship. He was raising three girls and one was already getting into trouble. Some people's dreams are fast, others stop and never begin again. Maybe that's what happened to my mother, or was it one of her sisters?

My father is not welcomed in my mother's house. He is from the wrong side of town. He is the wrong man. He has no father. He has little money. He has stepped off the train at the wrong stop. Is this what happens to your dreams? Maybe you are driving or riding and you miss your turn. Egberto Miller is on an express train and his destination is another dream. He wants another person to ride with him. Why be crushed alone by heavy blues? Share the pain and sorrow. Two trains running.

IV

Butter Ears, that's what we called Richard. My brother's ears were soft and great to touch. I loved to pull them. I would jump from behind the sofa or hide behind a door and when he passed I would grab his ears. Running away, I would make believe I was eating them, making funny noises in the back of my throat. If I was good my brother would let me play with his ears. I think Richard was the first person to open the door to my father's dreams. A baby boy born in 1943. The world is a terrible place to live. People are dying or being forced into camps as a baby boy searches for air and first words. Richard Egberto Miller. My father holds my brother by his middle name. This link, a name, would become a chain, a rope, something connecting one soul with another. Two train cars racing along a track.

In the cold December of 1942, before New Year's Eve, my father discovers prayer. He learns to bend his knees, to open his Bible to the first page. Genesis begins with the birth of his first child. The words are difficult to read but my father stumbles into the pleasure of language. He will keep this pleasure a secret from everyone. Not until after his death will the writer in the family discover this whisper, those markings in the holy book. Red checks and underlines like scars bleeding from one page into the next. In the dark Egberto reads and dreams about the baby boy to be born, his son and first light.

What would you do if you could create a man? Would you create a father or a son? Egberto thinks about the father he never saw, or saw but cannot remember. He dreams about becoming a father. He asks for God's blessing. God answers and then asks for his child. Is this why my brother became a monk? Was there a deal made? Who decided his journey? What would make a black boy growing up in the Bronx want to become a Trappist monk? When I ask my brother this question many years later, he quickly replies without hesitation that it was our father who drove him there. Becoming a monk was inevitable. Something was in his blood like music, Gregorian chants, Beethoven, Bach, Brahms, and Mozart wrestling with the jazz and the sounds of the Savoy.

While on his knees, Egberto Miller asks for God's

blessing. He wants his child to have more then he ever had. He promises to be a good father and never leave. It is 1943 and many people in the world are praying for their sons. Was God too busy too hear?

CHAPTER THREE

I

A child born on Good Friday is God's child. An old woman told my mother she was blessed for giving birth to Richard on the day Jesus died. Maybe this is just another story I remember hearing in Brooklyn after piano lessons. I don't know. Richard was my big brother. Long before black men would pass each other in the street and give strange handshakes, or simply nod in solidarity, I had a brother I was in love with. It was Richard whose spirit filled our house. His knowledge of classical music, Latin, animals, and sculpture gave color to our lives in the Bronx. It was my brother who now and then mentioned that he wanted to be pope. Dressed in sheets, blankets, or bathrobes, Richard knew how to part the Red Sea, feed the hungry, and be more holy than all the characters in those television movies shown around the Christmas holiday.

In his room, he built an altar. Two tall candles stood on each end. On the wall a large wooden crucifix. My father claimed it fell from the wall the day Richard returned from the monastery. I can believe it, because something died inside my brother when he returned home from upstate New York. His head had been shaven by monks.

What a surprise to come back from the grocery store and find my brother and father laughing like old friends. What secrets were they sharing? I stood between my sister and mother, separated from the men in my family.

I guess it started around the corner, behind the doors of St. Margaret Episcopal Church. Richard was an altar boy who held incense and candles for Father Kruger. The organ music would touch the top of the ceiling and press against the stained-glass windows. The Bible stories were better than cartoons and Dell comics before Marvel pushed them aside with the Metal Men. Somewhere between J.H.S. 52 and Morris High School, Richard would catch the faith like a cold. He joined the Catholic Church and ran the streets with his friend Ignacio. Ignacio was from Cuba and his family must have left the country when Fidel came to power. I would not even think about this until much later. My brother meanwhile was reading the writings of Thomas Merton in much the same manner as Julius Lester and Ernesto Cardenal. Around the world men were listening to their inner voices, leaving homes for solitude and the embracement of degrees of grace.

While I pulled on my brother's ears, something was tugging at his spirit. Although we were very close, Richard and I did none of the things brothers did. He hated sports and so we could not talk about whether Roberto Clemente was better than Willie Mays, or whether Warren Spahn threw a spitter. My brother was simply not interested. In many ways he reminded me of my father, except for his love of literature. It was Richard who borrowed and failed to return so many library books from the Hunts Point Library, that they sent an employee one Saturday to our home on Longwood Avenue. I answered the door and said I knew no one by the name of Richard Miller. My mother overheard my lie and made me search the house for books. Was this the first time I betrayed my brother?

II

My brother never talked to me about religion. Maybe it was because I was a girl who had no intention of becoming a nun. I saw many nuns in our neighborhood. You could see them around Fordham Road and Grand Concourse. Karen, my best friend, said the nuns could not dance; they didn't know how to move their bodies. She said the reason they prayed all day was because they could not dance. Not even to the twist and Chubby Checker. What would heaven be like without Sam Cooke and Percy Sledge?

Richard wanted to be a dancer. He liked ballet but my father said only girls danced that way and no son of his was going to wear tights in public. You would be called a he/she if you did. I asked my mother why Richard couldn't do what he wanted. She had no answers or explanations.

I thought Richard's room was strange with the altar and everything. I was always afraid of the candles and the fire. In his closet my brother kept his church robes. I liked the feel of them, the touch of silk on my flesh. Is this what Jesus wore? If he did a woman would believe in him. What a man wears can tell a woman many things. I thought my brother was becoming different from the person I chased in the Bronx Zoo. When we were seven and five and even ten and twelve we were very close. We shared every thing, toys, books, and clothes. But one day my brother became holy. There was no halo around his head or even a new look in his eyes. Richard just started reading more and playing the piano constantly. So maybe it was the music after all. When my brother refused to save his money to purchase records, that's when he cut himself off from the rest of us. He listened to that classical stuff. White music is what we called it. Karen and I thought the stuff was boring. It would make you dance funny or maybe not dance at all. It was the music that trapped my brother. Handel's *Messiah* was like a drug. What could you call Mozart and Bach? Richard would pretend he was a conductor and wave his hands in the air. My father encouraged my brother to pursue his love of music, even while his own head was filled with jazz. On the shelf in his closet would be those funny hats, the kind Ethelbert claimed Monk wore before he stopped talking. Leave it to my little brother to find something black in all this. Now that Richard and my father are both dead, it doesn't matter who influenced whom. I just wished I knew them better. All I have are stories and some of them might not even be true. Maybe my brother never became a monk. Maybe he was sent to reform school somewhere in upstate New York. I would like to think he didn't want to leave me. I was his sister and when we were young we were supposed to get married. Monks can't have wives. Didn't Richard know? Why did he lie and not tell me the truth? Why did he not confess? I was so angry with him when our family came back from LaGuardia Airport. My father had to go to work that day. My mother was so sad she didn't even go into the kitchen to fix his lunch. Instead I could hear her crying in the bedroom. I told my baby brother to stop making noise. He was too little to understand what had happened. Richard was gone. The same thing happened after his funeral.

III

Just before spring the first flowers bloom. They are beautiful yet very much alone. Like sentries they stand between seasons. This is how I think of my brother as I write *Fathering Words*. It is a warm February day and the earth is drying after a week of rain. I carry a few garbage bags out to the alley behind my house. In my backyard, the presence of white, yellow, and purple buds joined with the sounds of birds and the touch of a soft breeze. It is early morning, a Sunday, and I have the money in my pocket to purchase a newspaper. I will take a short walk and stop at a nearby store. My wife and children are asleep and so it is only me and these first flowers that try to speak to each other.

Sometimes a thing of beauty will remind me of my brother. Once it was just how the water of a river ran across the rocks in its bed. I stopped to look from a bridge and felt the enormous amount of grief pouring out from deep inside. This was just a few years ago, so the healing continues. The flowers appear and disappear like all things of beauty.

I never thought my brother would leave me. He never said anything about becoming a monk. Who did he talk to? My father? Mother? I don't remember any conversations during dinner. There were no brochures like the ones you get from the army and air force, on tables around the apartment. Please join God and see the world. No, my brother's departure was as sudden as someone's death. He put on his suit and tie and packed a bag. We got in the Dodge and went to the airport. We waved and came back home.

It was the early sixties and Richard was going north. In the South, the Civil Rights movement was at its peak. Young men and women were struggling to change America. A young James Baldwin spoke of love and fire. My brother left behind a copy of *Giovanni's Room* in his bookcase. My mother let me move my things into his room. The space, however, would remain Richard's during his entire stay at the monastery. I guess my mother knew he was coming back. No one else did. Everything was normal in our house even as outside the nation was being torn apart. What happens to families during civil wars? How do they fight and continue to love? Love and continue to fight?

Did my brother rebel against our parents? Was there an argument that I missed? Were they supportive of him because this was his dream, to become a monk? Did my father simply accept my brother's decision as a bad card given to him from the bottom of the deck? You grow up without a father and then you lose your son. Nothing but a bad joke. The bitterness could force the strongest man to mumble and turn his back on everything. I guess because my father didn't expect much in life it was easy for him to go to work every day without complaint. Or maybe it was the inner spirit, the contemplative soul who looks out the window and wonders about the meaning of life. If one is left alone, the purpose of life is supposed to become as clear as looking at flowers bloom.

My life consists of a medley of schools, P.S. 39 followed by the harsh rhythms of J.H.S. 120 (Paul Laurence Dunbar), Christopher Columbus High School, Howard University, UNLV, Emory & Henry College, Bennington

College and American University. A strange set of cloisters. Each place a step away from 938 Longwood Avenue in the Bronx. In the shadows of my father and brother, I grew for many years quietly in the shade like a vine reaching for daylight. In many ways I created myself. I learned from my father and brother the many ways to disguise sadness and loneliness.

I grew up without a room, a space to call my own. I was given the hallway closet for my books and toys. I had only one or two friends. Dinky and Judy. We played baseball even in winter when there was snow on the ground. Dinky was rumored to be a cousin. His family lived upstairs and members would sometime come into our apartment without knocking. So I guess we were all related. We knew people who had accents and talked about the West Indian islands as if they were places in the Bible. Judy was my girlfriend and she was Chinese. Her cousin Eva's family operated a laundry not far from school. My early writing consisted of love letters to Judy with my name and a few questions. Do you love me? I love you. Judy's replies would be the only statement I would get in writing until Michelle stopped me on the campus of Howard and asked for directions to the bookstore.

Maybe I should have been given away when I was a child. I could have been raised in Brooklyn, or Queens. Someplace with a backyard and green grass. My room would be the attic. Sun would come in and dance the way my sister did. My family was working class. We had no contact with the black middle class except when we went to see Auntie, my great aunt who lived on what was once called Sugar Hill. Years later the black history courses I took and the books I read would provide a map to the discoveries during my childhood years. I was the type of child who read books, did poorly in math, excellent in social studies, and was the second fastest runner in my class. Throughout my life I was always the runner-up. Second place. Silver medal. No gold or endorsements.

To my mother and father it was Richard who was the son. I was the third child, like a third strike chasing the corner of the plate. A sudden surprise. Everyone is caught looking at the new addition to the family. On occasions when we visited Brooklyn as a family, to join relatives who still had their accents, someone would say to my mother, "Enid, when did you have another child?" This would usually cause some laughter throughout the room. My mother seldom said anything. It was as if the joke was the reminder of a botched abortion.

Both of my parents were always excited about what my brother did. It must have started with his first baby steps and words. I can see my brother crawling around on the floor with my father taking pictures. Richard was the handsome child, his hair different from my own as well as Marie's. It was Richard my father wanted to show off to the world.

A man walks along a beach, turns around, and notices his footsteps for the first time. This is how I can best describe my father as a new father. Richard, his first born, a dream he has no problem waking up to feed.

Today I was thinking about the responsibilities of fatherhood. I have never worked a day as hard as my father. If my shoulder or back hurts, it is from spending too many hours at the computer. It does not come from lifting boxes and packages, sorting mail, trying to catch a train in the wee hours of the morning. My father walked down dark streets with his money tucked away in a secret place. How many times was he stopped, robbed, or had his life threatened? As I write *Fathering Words,* I think of my own life, so much different from my father's. Is it a result of mastering the word? Is this what Frederick Douglass realized? The discovery of reading and writing can be linked to freedom.

I live a writer's life, surrounded by books, ideas, and yes, dreams. What I am doing right now is trying to describe my footsteps. How did I get here? What did I discover as well as lose along the way? I had a conversation with my agent yesterday about what this book was going to be. "Where was the narrative?" she asked. People need a straight narrative. I thought of the flowers blooming in my backyard. How they suddenly appeared one day after the rain. Their petals flutter in the wind. How sad they look when the weather changes, the cold air encouraging them to return to the earth.

I want to reclaim memory, to feel the ground beneath my feet. The telling of this story must be woven like a quilt. The parts taken from the past, present, and future. The words exist all at once. The life of my brother, father, and I are small patches resting next to each other. This is what I thought when I stood looking at their graves a few years ago. Men reduced to ashes, pieces of men becoming memories. It is the word, the tale, the story that survives. It is the combination of history and myth that creates this book.

I am inside my father's dream. We are coming to America. This will be our beginning. Even before I am born I search for words, for a consciousness. I cross the water with a man who will one day let me breathe. These words today splash against the rocks of time. Each wave returns me to the past and pulls me toward the future. The making of this quilt is like embracing an ocean. How can I wrap my arms around so much water?

CHAPTER FOUR

I

$\mathcal{B}$ecause I was a girl, I knew my father better than my brothers. Of course it wasn't until I was divorced and he was sick. Taking care of an older person can heal a young heart. One discovers patience and other things that were on the shelf or in the medicine cabinet. When I was younger I learned to love my father, a man I once feared while growing up. I would stand by his bedroom door, looking at his body rise and fall with each breath. I guess I never wanted to have children because of what my father told me. Even when I married and became Marie Hunter, I kept my father's words of wisdom around like a night-light. How else could I survive the Bronx?

II

Before rap music came out of the South Bronx, one could hear Puerto Ricans and African Americans playing their drums in the summertime. The year before I went off to college, I knew my inability to dance saved me from running with the wrong crowd. My parents kept my brother, sister, and me off the streets. Only when we were older did we realize that we had avoided jail, pregnancy, death, and the scars that come with early adulthood. If my brother was saved by candles, holy water, and religion, then it was the "glove" that allowed me to survive the housing projects and killing fields.

I was very good at playing baseball. My signature move was leaping against a fence, sticking my glove out over it, and taking away homers. I liked to hang on the fence, giving the hitter the impression I had missed the baseball. As soon as I spotted the home run trot, the swagger, the clapping of the hands, the boast or yell, then like a magician I would stick my glove up showing the ball to all. When I wasn't running down balls in the outfield, I was playing third base. Since I was a New York Yankee fan, the person I always wanted to be was Clete Boyer. Boyer was known for diving and backhanding a hard liner down the line and throwing the hitter out from his knees. How many times did I try to do this? Was this as close as I would come to prayer?

Once I caught my father kneeling, praying in his bedroom. It was before he was to have an operation on his lungs. I was still in college, home for a few days. The house was like Yankee Stadium after the loss of a close game. Everyone was caught in the moment of thinking about their performance. How could they lose? My mother, always a pillar of strength, had been picked off first base and caught in a rundown. How could she live without my father? Who would provide for the family? We were running toward second when my father became sick.

My mother and sister confronted me about school. You better get a job or come home. Don't be wasting our money with this foolish idea about becoming a writer. We didn't send you off to college to do that. Don't you see that your father is sick?

It must have been this same argument or knife that my mother stuck in my brother's back when he was at the monastery. Did she write letter after letter encouraging him to come home? Your father is having problems; come home, if you can. There were things my father was unaware of taking place in the kitchen, the living room, in his own house.

The streets, however, were something my father knew about, and this knowledge he passed on to his children like recorded revelations creating a new holy book. Somewhere the recorded texts of how to deal with women became the "lost" Scripture. Unless, I could decipher the many things my father said about my mother, it would be impossible to understand how he survived. Each pearl of wisdom that fell from his mouth was often delivered while he was propped up in bed, the television channel stuck on some western like *Bonanza* or *Gunsmoke*. The entire room dark except for the screen. The Pan-African intellectual C. L. R. James would hold court in a much similar manner, but I would encounter his genius much later on my journey toward becoming a writer. Egberto Miller shifts in his bed as my feet dangle off the end. We could be two people on a raft. Lost at sea; food running out as well as our trust and tempers. Yet we are dependent on each other like piano and bass players or pitchers and catchers.

"I could leave your mother and be like everyone else," my father says to me during a commercial. It doesn't matter how old I am, his words will find a place in the cuff of my pants, in the corner of my coat pocket, or as I turn a corner on a cold winter afternoon and turn my collar up against the wind. My father is blowing down my neck like

Coleman Hawkins, and someone says, "The Hawk is blowing," and the notes from my father's life are rushing at me and the composition is as complex as anything Thelonious Monk could imagine. Yes, "Ruby My Dear."

Two bodies in the dark, one talking and the other listening to a strange sound coming from where pain and hurt is mixed with depression and the blues, and if you cry for everyone and not just yourself, this is where you discover the Middle Passage, the Holocaust, the plantation, the concentration camps, the bombing of cities, and whatever is left. This is the howl Allen Ginsberg described for an entire generation. That spoken unspokeness. Those moments between father and son that are not the simplicity of playing catch with a ball and glove. It is the moment when your father lets you touch the nakedness of his back. The place where the weight of his own sex and identity meets your own. And the mirror you were afraid to look into is the face of your own father, and this is also the face of history.

III

My father never said he loved me. Only his presence every day while I was a child reminded me that words have their limitations. What a strange thing for a writer to learn. My father learned his lesson when he met my mother's father. What could he say? I met your daughter dancing at the Savoy. Can I marry her? What did my grandfather know about love? Here was a man trying to raise three daughters and failing at the job. He once moved to Long Island to get away from the black boys who roamed the streets looking for a skirt to raise in the name of love. My mother's sister Winnie got caught, and this was the beginning of a cold war a few years before Churchill talked about the Iron Curtain and my grandfather closed his door to everyone, especially my father.

When Egberto married Enid, Edgerton Marshall, my grandfather did not bless the union. He did not even give a wedding gift. In the early days of my father's marriage, my mother must have questioned her choice. Did she make the right decision? What was it about this quiet man? Yes, he was handsome and yes, his hands were soft and his eyes clear. Was this the movies? In the pictures I have of my mother when she is in her late twenties and early thirties, her hair is in the style of those women who played roles opposite Bogart and Gable. I see my mother leaning against the window like Lena Horne. She is singing something like "Stormy Weather" and Katherine Dunham is dancing somewhere as far away as where my father was born.

Man to man. My father would dislike my grandfather his entire life. When things were going poorly in our house, when money was short, my mother would talk to herself, mumble words that blamed herself for the situation she was in. All the things she wanted or dreamed about she knew she was never going to have. In her heart she also decided that if she couldn't have what she wanted, no one else would, and this included everyone she fixed a meal for while standing on feet with swollen ankles.

All through my youth, my Bronx childhood, I don't recall any real arguments between my parents. All I remember hearing was the soft static of mumbling coming from the bedroom, bathroom, or kitchen. This is how my mother and father communicated with each other. Mumbling. A domestic form of scat singing. Like Ella and Cab, my parents would run out of words. My grandfather refused to listen to jazz, so my father, like Dizzy and Bird, created a new sound. Gone was the big band and the close ties to West Indians living in Brooklyn. My father started a small band in the Bronx. When my brother learned to play the piano, folks claimed that he would be another Bud Powell, but then Richard went classical and my father was like Ellington the night Billy Strayhorn died.

When you can't find love, your heart stops and listens to music. You walk out of your house and you can't decide which way to go. So you wait for your ears to lead your eyes. When you hear the jazz or the blues, it doesn't matter how much money you have in your pocket. It's not enough to explain how Egberto feels. All he knows is that he can't stay where he is. Egberto is Langston Hughes in search of the big sea. So he turns around to catch the train back to the other side of town. If he looks over his shoulder, he will lose Enid forever. Something makes him turn around, a mumbling, a distant sound forever coming from the future. What was the name of that song at the Savoy? Why did my grandfather dislike the music so much? Why was my mother always telling my father not to play jazz in the house. My mother mysteriously claiming the music was awful, that it was noise. I write, looking back over my shoulder at my mother. I know I'm losing her.

CHAPTER FIVE

I

Maybe, because I was a girl I knew my mother better then my brothers. My mother wanted to become a nurse. It was just a girlhood dream she had while growing up and working in a war factory. Many people have dreams when they see the door locked or closing in front of them. Enid Miller was no different. She was standing against a wall when a shy guy asked her to dance. If it was me, I would have been on the dance floor, trying my best to mess up my hair.

When I got married I had the biggest wedding in the St. Mary's Projects. It was one of those moments when my mother remembered her first kiss. I had been reading magazines for years, waiting for the right guy to ride a white horse into the projects without getting mugged. I think my mother gave me away instead of my father. I was her big girl, the one child she could shape in her own image.

II

So many images in my poems have my mother's hair and hands. My mother worked in the garment industry in New York. She did piece work. Cutting and sewing. Rhinestones would sparkle in front of her eyes and she would blink again and again. Yet even with her eyes closed she could catch you stealing a cookie or not washing behind your ears. Enid's eyes would make you confess before you did something wrong. Her hands were those of a working woman, the softness only found in what they had accomplished.

I was not aware of how controlling my mother's hands were until I tried to escape. It was my mother's hands that I seldom saw my father hold. It was my brother who was always bringing something home to place in those hands. Often it was flowers she would receive at the door, smelling them first and then looking around to find her favorite vase. My sister received instructions for womanhood from my mother's hands. How to cook, fix hair, oil one's legs, and sew. Were these wonderful hands the ones that wanted to give me away?

It is 1968, and the world seems to be coming apart. Martin Luther King Jr. and Robert Kennedy are killed. Students are in the streets of Paris. At Howard University in Washington, young people closed the school. Riots across America and the Vietnam War outside. I was listening to Hendrix, Dylan, Simon and Garfunkel and the Chambers Brothers. I graduated from Christopher Columbus High School in early January and took a job at Bookazine down on Christopher Street. I was attempting to earn and save a few dollars before I went off to college in September. It wasn't certain that I would go. My mother had the final say in these matters. If she agreed to let me attend Howard University, then she was willing to let me do something that she prohibited my brother or sister to do. Would she permit one child to live out on the frontier, beyond her sight?

My brother had returned a few years earlier from a Trappist monastery in New York State. He was working at Bankers Trust and hating every day of it. This was purgatory turning into hell. Richard's only salvation was in his music and the playing of the organ on Sundays at a church in Brooklyn. His life had become some medieval tale. It was as if my brother had been banished back into a world of trolls and demons. In his apartment in Manhattan, near Riverside Drive, not far from Grant's tomb, he filled his rooms with sculpture and paintings. He had a cat and then a dog, for he loved animals as much as Saint Francis. My brother's place was always dark, the side street only permitting enough light to sketch the outside of his moods. But this was a place I loved to visit. When I was in high school and college I would drop by my brother's apartment. Here we would laugh, talk about family, current affairs, and our destinies. Richard was heavy into prophecy and how he would return in another life and get his due.

On the days we would decide to take the train down to Greenwich Village to shop in the bookstores, we would often pass my brother's friend Carmen on the street. Her eyes would catch the light for just a moment and her face would glow and she would make a small bow in my brother's direction. Carmen believed my brother was a saint and that his life had special meaning. In 1985, she would tell me this again. Her story would become the beginning of a book.

III

A season in baseball can be long or short. It depends on the team, as well as one's personal records. If you're hitting good, time passes very quickly. A road trip ends and suddenly you're back home. I was happy in 1968 to go off to college. I had never seen Howard University or been to Washington, D.C.

On the day I left with my mother and Aunt Evelyn, my father had not return home from work. It was only when we had reached the subway station that he appeared on the other side of the tracks. He waved good-bye to me as if I was a tourist. What was he thinking? Had he seen this all before? A family member waving and then departing. The separation by tracks and the first lines of a blues tune can be heard on this early morning. Or maybe it's Martin Luther King Jr. leaning over a balcony in Memphis asking someone to play "Precious Lord" one more time.

The loneliness of leaders and fathers. A family of followers, so close but still so far away to touch or really ever know. My father said nothing to me prior to going off to college. He didn't watch me pack or offer advice about how to live away from home. I was on my own. There was a feeling inside of me of joy and happiness. I was escaping to a city I had never seen. Washington, D.C., was simply the White House to me, nothing else. I had no understanding of the fact that I was traveling south. I was moving backward into history and Howard. I was joining the middle class and colored society filled with fraternities and sororities. I was lining up to become a doctor, dentist, or lawyer. I was going from the projects to a place the great negritude poet Leon Damas once called a plantation. Of course we were standing outside in the shadow of the college library laughing at ourselves, the sun setting on our blackness but not our sense of humor.

Did Dorothy ever stop to describe Oz? I am suddenly a tall, slender, young black kid living in the same room with Brad, who was a hoodlum from New York. Cook Hall, and I am sharing a room smaller than the one I did with my brother. There are no candles burning. Only the burning anger and hatred between myself and Brad. There will come nights where we exchange blows and must be separated by men who are now making money quietly or running for political office in cities still rebuilding from the riots.

Brad and his buddies were drug users and thieves. I don't remember their graduating in the early seventies. Once they stole the carpet out of the lounge of one of the dormitories. They laughed about this for days while the administration sent around a memo informing us to be careful of the people in the surrounding community. I lay in my bed one night looking at Brad and one of his friends who had moved in with us. One night while working in a factory as a maintenance man, my father was tied up by two robbers. Brad and his friend could be their children. Bad luck can follow a family around like they were the Kennedys. Since I was the baby of the family I was sheltered from many awful experiences until this trip south to college.

The one thing about having a horrible roommate is that you begin to spend more time outside your room. I lived in Cook Hall, across from the football field and near Cramton Auditorium. Cook Hall was the best male dorm to live in with its double courtyards and different sections. The rooms needed painting. They had a military look or maybe they served as a reminder that the year before I was enrolled, ROTC was mandatory for all males. The student protest movement before my arrival abolished this requirement. Brad would have made a nice drill sergeant. I would have gone AWOL by the third week.

IV

I remember Richard going off to the monastery, but I don't remember my baby brother going off to college. I was in nursing school, something my mother was always telling someone else about. I think she started living my life around then. She was happy that Richard was working in a bank, making what she called "good money." My father had steady work at the post office. A person's world consisted of moons and stars. Enid was the center of everything. If her children were to shine, they would have to reflect her light. My brother, who attempted to light his own candles, was thrown into darkness as soon as he returned home from the monastery. That's what my baby brother believed. I think it's nonsense. We were all happy when we moved into the St. Mary's Projects and had more room. One's own space is very important. I tell my patients, if they can afford a single room in the hospital, be sure to get it. Nothing is worse than being sick and sick of the person in the bed next to you. Why would anyone want a roommate anyway. My divorce was the best thing that ever happened to me.

V

So far away was New York that I stopped thinking about it. College was like exile or some strange migration I had made without any reason except maybe to escape a war or famine. I left behind no girlfriend. No lover. I made few telephone calls home but I did write letters. How it started I don't know. But by my second semester at Howard I was a frequent visitor to the post office to obtain letters and stamps. When you go away you're suppose to write. Drop a note or postcard. Let folks know you're well. Who you write says a lot about who you love.

Four years in college and not one letter to my father. What does that say? It was so difficult to connect with him. I wanted to but could never find the words. The letters I received from my mother were quick notes wrapped around money. My mother had developed a form of shorthand she must have learned during the war. Keep it brief so the enemy won't discover one's location.

VI

Going off to college, leaving the South Bronx, was the first step in my own migration. In many ways I was following in the footsteps of the men in my family. Departure and farewell. My father, a young boy coming to America, my brother taking an airplane to join a community of monks in upstate New York. We leave one place for another. I don't know how I made it to college. I filled out applications to attend Hartwick College, Columbia University, and Howard. Why Hartwick? The brochures described a large campus with trees. I guess I wanted to get away from the city. I knew that as soon as I got a ticket I would never return. Going off to college was "one way" in much the same way as the Underground Railroad was. I was escaping the arms of my mother and preventing the loss of my dreams. I was unaware of how much I was influenced by the sadness trapped within the lives of my brother and father.

Why Howard? The one black teacher at Columbus High School (who taught physics) recommended Howard. I had never heard of it. It was outside my imagination. A place where everyone is black. How could this be?

My second week on campus I went to a Ujamaa meeting. Attending were a militant group of students who had been active in the recent student protests. I sat in the student center listening to speeches about blackness and one's responsibility to the black community. After someone introduced Judy Howell to the audience, nothing made sense to me. Judy was the neighborhood community activist assigned to the Howard campus to make students feel weak, immature, and not ready for the revolution. Here was the Bronx neighborhood bad girl who had once stolen my baseball glove. How strange to make it all the way to college only to be haunted by a bad memory from childhood. I looked at Judy as if she was a figure out of Greek mythology. Would I be cursed to spend four years on a college campus with her? Thirty? How could I free myself? What protection would I need to survive?

I came to Howard University to find a wife. I told members of my family that I wanted to become a lawyer. Was this a lie? With the exception of one girl in the fourth grade, my relationship with women was limited to opening and holding doors. I was the perfect gentleman. When I had completed packing for college, my mother provided me with one bit of advice. "Don't let anyone tell you it's yours" she said, while washing dishes one evening. I had no idea

42

what she was talking about. Little did I know this was my sex education reduced down to an expression. There was no video tape, no package of rubbers.

The same problems I had with mathematics, I had with women. How come I could never get the right answer? Sex was like calculus. It was something other students were doing. I had been left behind with basic algebra and a notebook.

However, when I listened to Judy Howell address the gathering of potential black militants, I knew there was no time for romance. I had to prepare for the revolution, study hard, and obtain nation-building skills. I had yet to meet the guys who would be talking about polygamy and practicing home-brewed Islam, the men who sold incense to the ladies at half-price and invited them to the community mosque only to tell them that marriage was half the faith. I was a slow learner and there were many things to learn on the campus of Howard University.

I can't remember when I started writing letters to my brother in New York. It might have been the second semester. I do know some of these letters contained small poems of my personal feelings placed on paper. There were numerous references to blackness and to the daily observations I had started to record. My birth as a writer was "accidental." Almost like meeting my new roommate, Reggie Hudgins, from Philadelphia. It's strange how one's life can be affected by people you don't know. A person rubs sleep from his eyes, pushes back the covers, searches for slippers, walks to the bathroom, and turns the toilet seat up. In the quiet of the morning only the sound of urine hitting water can be heard. What will happen in the next two or three hours is impossible to determine. This is how poetry begins.

CHAPTER SIX

I

Langston Hughes did not live in Cook Hall. I was the only poet in a dorm filled with future doctors, lawyers, preachers, teachers, government workers, musicians, dentists, soldiers, lovers, drug addicts, crazy Negroes, Muslims, Republicans, gays, and guys who would see you every day and not speak. It was not the best place to become a writer. I should have left Howard like Langston left Columbia. Would I have thrown my books into the ocean? Nineteen sixty-eight and the nation is bleeding from too many wounds. I am in a classroom trying to take notes and pay attention. Margaret, a small girl from Newport News, kisses me and turns my mouth to paper. I am filled with words. Is this poetry?

At night small fragments begin to breathe. I like the feel of creating something. My father taught me how to sketch, to make shapes, to turn circles into faces. Add a nose, two eyes, and ears. Poetry is like drawing. I find a line I like and turn it over and over in my head. I stretch the words, bend them, place them on the page, change them again. I enjoy this more then going to class.

I begin to think about blackness. Not the color of my

skin but the color of ideas. Fanon, Nkrumah, DuBois are new names for me. I am learning how to swim in a big sea. So much to learn, to study, to read and talk about. College, so far from the housing projects in the Bronx. I hold a black book in my hand filled with the history of my people. I had none of this growing up. My father only used the word "colored." He never said black or Negro, only colored. This was as late as 1987. Egberto Miller died during Black History Month, on February 2nd. He died after the birthday of Langston Hughes. My father had his funeral where Langston had his—Benta's Funeral Home in Harlem. Coincidence? But then what is black history but a series of coincidences that run parallel to everything in the universe.

There are days when I don't attend class. If the weather is warm, the main courtyard is crowded. Students standing around in front of Douglass Hall or sitting on the wall down by the Women's Quadrangle. If Langston were here he would be looking for the production of "Shuffle Along" and some crazy woman like Zora. Margaret is not Zora. She is the first woman I decide to see or maybe just talk to. I met her and her roommates on the freshman boat ride, girls from towns in the South I had never heard of and couldn't spell. What did we have in common? What if I had sex and one of these coeds got pregnant?

Would their parents suddenly appear on a Saturday morning before the term ended, tell me to pack my footlocker and get in the car parked in front the dorm? The car with the southern tags. Before hitting the first red light, my mother's face would appear in the rearview mirror or above a traffic light. She would be wearing one of those "I told you so" expressions.

Living away from home for the first time, I am haunted by my mother's image. I have freedom but also invisible chains. I see some of my friends doing things they would never do at home: drugs, sex, running with the wrong crowd. There are so many different groups of students at Howard. The militants, the frats, the professional students who are pre-med and pre-law and pretty predictable. There are the student government folks, the athletes, and yes, the party people. The bad rap on Howard was that it was a party school and not a place for serious intellectual growth and opportunities. I saw both during the early school days or was it daze? If Spike Lee had been making movies during my freshman year, all my friends would have had roles.

I decided to run back and forth between the student government, pre–Black Caucus groupies, and the militants, some who were also artists. I was shocked one day to discover Jomo, our best militant, using a hall phone in Cook Hall to read some verse he had written to his girlfriend. A sister, I guess, who had become his Nile Nubian queen and had invested in early African fabric from a community store. And, of course, there was my friend Michael Harris, who had been one of the student leaders of the takeover of the administration building at Howard in the spring of 1968. Michael was from Chicago, and was smart enough to realize that you could be a celebrity without going to class. I had been introduced to his reputation when I saw the television documentary "Color Us Black" back in New York. It was that film that made me want to paint myself red, black, and green. Michael was always walking around the campus reciting the poem "Warning" by Langston Hughes. It was what I considered a radical poem. My knowledge of other compositions would grow as I became more aware of black history, black poetry, and the Black Arts movement. But first I had to find a wife.

II

Are Negro girls getting prettier? *Ebony* magazine once posed that question around the time I was going off to college. It's the type of strange things that take place in the editorial rooms of many major black publications. Why do they all begin with the letter *E*? *Ebony, Essence, Emerge, Encore, Elan.* What's up with that? E. Ethelbert Miller. What does the *E* stand for? A magazine?

I changed my name my sophomore year at Howard. I reinvented myself. Maybe everything I am writing now is a continuation of that 1969 decision, like the Brown, Supreme Court decision of 1954. I was Gene to my parents, especially my father. I enrolled in college as Eugene E. Miller, but like the legal blow against segregation, I became more social and outgoing under the name E. Ethelbert Miller.

How did it happen? Was it as quick as my grandmother changing my father's last name from Williams to Miller when they came to America? A new identity, an escape as good as anything Houdini could do. The magic was first discovered in the lounge of Drew Hall. A number of us were thinking about running for student government as a ticket. I was selected to run for freshman class treasurer. It was obvious that no one had checked my poor math grades from elementary to high school. A consecutive record of failures with numbers that established a Ripken-like streak. The person handling my campaign was a young coed from Chicago. She had a nice afro and shape, and she was funny and smart. We sat on the floor in the lounge trying to come up with slogans for posters and we couldn't. She asked about my middle name. Ethelbert, I told her, and she laughed. She came up with this silly expression about "Ethelbert Is Coming" and soon made posters with an airplane, which struck me as stupid but what did I know about politics. Many students found the expression funny and voted for me and I won. So I was Eugene Ethelbert Miller after a few weeks away from the Bronx. But folks would call me Eugene until I ran for sophomore class president and decided to cast myself as a new politician. I had resigned from being freshman class treasurer because I refused to spend money on a class party and folks wanted to party and so they did so without me. Just as Richard Nixon became the new Nixon to some, I changed my name to E. Ethelbert Miller. On campus around this time was a white postgraduate student studying African American literature and his name was Eugene E. Miller. We spoke and laughed about our names. When I went to pay my tuition, I was told that it had been paid, but I told them the money belonged to the other Eugene Miller.

No matter what I had changed my name to, I was still my father's son. I was the first person in my family to go to college. My father's long days and nights made it possible for me to escape from New York. We never talked about school, how it was, or what I was studying. My father never sent me a note or card. When I returned home during Thanksgiving, Christmas, or the semester break, there was nothing but silence between us. No dinner conversations, or long walks and confessions.

I knew my middle name was something my father had nothing to do with. My mother got the idea from her great aunt, the same one she almost gave me away to. I did not learn this secret until years later and then my mother and sister would say that I made it up. But who could believe them? They were women who shared moments in kitchens and bathrooms. Their hands handled food and soap. It was my mother who every two weeks sent a few dollars in the mail to my campus box. She was still working now and then in the garment industry, her eyes and hands beginning to slow down as she sewed. No lie can be as straight as a needle.

III

*E*ven when he was in college I called him Monkey Gene. Gene the Monkey. I don't know why he decided to go to Howard. Where was that? Nobody we knew ever went there. It was either City College, Brooklyn College, or Hunter College. I wanted to be a nurse so I stayed in New York. I had the blessings of my mother. It was her dream to be a nurse. We seldom talked about what we wanted to be when we lived on Longwood Avenue, and so I didn't know I was living my mother's life until I discovered my own. That came after marriage and divorce and the joy of living by myself in Yonkers.

I thought the entire name change thing was as crazy as getting an afro, or wearing African clothes, or going to Africa. E. Ethelbert Miller, please! What was he getting into down in Washington? All that black stuff was crazy. I saw it on television. It didn't have anything to do with my life. When you're thinking about working in a hospital all you see is red, the color of blood. Folks don't have no time for race relations when they are sick or dying; and why didn't my brother take an African name if he wanted to be so black and different? He could have been Kwame, or one of those principles associated with that thing called Kwanzaa. You know, he could have called himself Umoja or something like that.

He sent a few poems to Richard. I never saw them but Richard said they were funny. I thought it was a waste of money for him to be away at school writing poetry. Our parents weren't millionaires, and when daddy got sick I told him he better be thinking about something that was going to pay the rent. Nobody wants to be around a poor colored man, even if he thinks he's black.

CHAPTER SEVEN

I

A student would kill for a single room. A room of one's own. Enter Cook Hall, Room 288. I could be Bud Powell. Here I am trying to be an artist and the dorm is filled with people who don't understand my music. Like my father and brother, I finally have my four walls. From the second semester of my sophomore year until graduation, I lived in a single room painted maybe by the U.S. Army. My walls were ocean green; one day I covered them with aluminum foil and almost blinded myself when I turned on the overhead lights. On another occasion I decorated my room with pages from *The Village Voice*, hung a huge American flag upside down in the symbol of distress. I did not recognize some of the symptoms of depression or the shadows of Richard and Egberto in the corner of my room when I closed the door.

It was here that I became a writer. Confined to a small place, attending just enough classes to maintain a decent grade average. I started on the journey toward creating myself, finding that identity lost somewhere inside words and stories. So what if Bud Powell thought he could fly? Was Charlie Parker not called Bird? My sister calling me Monkey Gene and not Monk? The complexity of the coming of age. New chords and arrangements.

In my small, monastic room I created my world. I had more books than the typical student. A number of people borrowed books for leisure reading and reports. My reputation on campus grew. Somewhere my voice as a writer would slowly emerge from its cave and hibernation.

What seeds were responsible for my harvest? My first words sprouted out from the lyrics of Paul Simon, Bob Dylan, Phil Ochs, and the folk rock musicians of the sixties. I liked the voice that was alienated, the singer or bard who sang out of loneliness and pain. The personal blues of disappointment, lost love, and innocence. I had purchased a guitar once but only learned how to play a few notes of Simon's "The Sounds of Silence." I like the images found in Dylan's "Memphis Blues" and made his song "Tamborine Man" almost my anthem. At Howard, however, the sounds of Dylan collided with the music of the Delfonics and the Dells.

The move from the Bronx to Washington was a cultural leap for me into a predominately black world. Music is like blood, flowing or perhaps dripping at times. Dylan and not Dunbar influenced my muse. But this would change with a few good teachers like Jennifer Jordan, Bill Thomas, and Stephen Henderson. I was still trying to comprehend what was happening to me while the rest of the world was in turmoil. What kept me awake at night? After I moved out of my room with Brad, I shared a space for a semester with Reggie, but by my second year I had a coveted single room. A writer's room?

On envelopes to my friend Dinky, who had enrolled at Columbia, I began to write short poems. Others I would send to my brother. Many were about the contradictions I was experiencing around me. How black was Howard?

When was the revolution coming? I was like a young Baldwin walking across campus as if it were the streets of Harlem. Someone would come into my room, examine my record collection, and dismiss me as a traitor to the race. How could I listen to white music? I would hold up a Hendrix album and they would laugh, and I felt I was an alien many galaxies away from the music of Sun Ra and his Arkestra. So few of us could see the future in 1969.

And then it happened without any warning or announcement. The future was Michelle Calhoun from Chicago. I had seen her from a distance but had only nodded. She left many guys speechless and spinning like tops. You had to turn around when she passed. Michelle was beautiful beyond the ten fingers on my hand. How could anyone just think about spending one night with her when so many others wanted to give their lives. If Michelle was music, then she was Holiday with flowers and Ella making up words so that you could speak.

On an overcast Saturday, where the McMillan Reservoir embraces Fourth Street in the crook of an arm, I saw her walking alone. She was wearing a long, brown coat and wool hat. It might have been late September or early October. It was a time when leaves change and fall beckons, the warm air turning cold. I am crossing in the middle of the street, heading back to Cook Hall after talking with a friend in the Women's Quadrangle. I see Michelle and she is the only person walking on this street that is about to connect our lives. She is not standing against the wall of the Savoy waiting to dance. Michelle is walking toward me and she is smiling, and I don't even know her name yet. Her face and the rest of her is the door to every dream I have ever dreamt. This is my education, my graduation all coming together at once. What if I fail?

If I were to write the script, what would be the magic

words? Boy meets girl. What does he say? What's his opening line? OK . . . it's just a poetic moment. Snag the image. Now what? Keep it simple. "Hi."

Michelle wants to know if the campus bookstore is open on Saturday. Bookstore? Saturday? The hours? What I loved about Joe Montana when he was quarterbacking the 49ers was that quick ability he had to read the defense and call the audible. I hear Michelle's question before the ball is snapped, and I respond, "I don't know . . . let's go see." My life is changed forever. This is the first time I've written it down. Touchdown, baby!

II

If I had not met Michelle, I would never have met the black poet Don L. Lee. I was unaware he was teaching a class in Douglass Hall. Like comic strip lovers, Michelle and I began doing everything together. I followed her to class one day. Tall, light complexion, thin, and handsome. Lee was from Chicago, the same city as Michelle. On this day he was teaching with the help of a cheap, white, portable record player. It's the kind your parents buy for you before you start listening to music in any serious manner. Or maybe I saw one of these things when I was in elementary school and the teacher kept it on the back shelf next to the goldfish bowl. No need to lock the record player in the closet; no one is going to steal it. Lee is playing "Stay In My Corner" by the Dells. He closed his eyes and one could see him slow dancing in a basement on the Southside of the city by the lake. "This is real poetry" he tells the class. Yes, I agree. This is better than Dylan, especially with Michelle sitting next to me singing the words. Yes, please stay in my corner, baby. Stay. I know we are both young

56

and you're engaged to some boy back home, but—Stay. Yes, I don't know what I should major in and don't have a clue to what kind of job I want, but—Stay. You're the first woman I will ever make love to, so—Stay. I know what the future will bring because time has passed and I'm writing all of this, so—Stay. When you said you wanted to leave, I let you go. But right now we are young, the song is so sweet and precious, so—Stay. And yes, this might not have ever happened, but it did and I'm so happy. Even now as I write I know I could end it here. I could stay in my corner. Like my father—Stayed. I could stay in my corner. Like my brother—Stayed. Yes, with just a kiss from you I would stay.

III

On the path to love or becoming, one should have a mentor. Self-help books can only contribute so much. Two years into my college education and I still thought it was freshman week. Finding a woman like Michelle, whom I affectionately call Mickey, was the first of many blessings. Next door to me in room 289, lived Steve Jones, who perhaps was another witness to the mysterious ways of the Lord. Steve was an older student. He was funny and thought that many of us in the dorm needed to grow up before we took seriously the idea of being black. Steve was into black culture with footnotes. I was still doing the Negro History Week quiz.

Although he was studying architecture at Howard he found time to perform in plays held around town. One such play was the *Militant Black Preacher* written by Ben Caldwell. Steve performed this play at All Souls Church located on the corner of Sixteenth and Harvard Streets.

The play was directed by the elusive Bob Stokes. Bob was as generous as he was mysterious. He was always doing something. When I met him he was operating a community black theater company on hardly any funds. Set designs were developed out of what he found in alleys. He kept a bass in a mostly vacant apartment not too far from campus. Steve introduced me to Bob when he came by the dorm one evening. I had been writing a few poems, sending them to the school newspaper, sharing a few with friends. Bob seemed to take note of this but said very little to me.

So many children are sent off to college to pursue an education that hopefully will result in a good job, house, neighborhood, and bright kids of their own. This is a ritual and journey repeated every September. The idea of finding a master teacher or mentor is often not discussed. While waiting on line to register for classes one might ask another student about what teacher to take, what classes are easy, who grades on a curve, and whether or not a person can sleep by the door or in the back of the room. Now and then one encounters a master teacher, the person who makes a dull subject come to life. That's the teacher who makes you shout in Greek when reading the classics or encourages you to drop your books and follow Tubman to freedom. The master teacher has the reputation that is upheld by scholarship and intimidation. This teacher is capable of throwing the Major League curve, the type of thing you never saw in high school. Yes, it comes on a straight line aimed right at your head and then it drops over the plate for a strike, and your understanding is now knowledge and you cannot forget what you just learned or witnessed.

One can walk the earth, including the inner cities, and not encounter a mentor. No, I am not talking about role models and sneakers. It's not about being like Mike. It's about discovering oneself while another holds a mirror for you to see into your heart. If you have dreams, the mentor will point you in the right direction. A map of your journey will be found inside of yourself.

Months after our first meeting, Bob Stokes stopped Michelle and me across the street from Cramton Auditorium and asked if I was still writing poetry. Around this time the Mets won the World Series and other unnatural occurrences would take place. The Black Panthers would be growling across America at the FBI, and Stokley Carmichael was just about ready to take Black Power to that next level of Pan-Africanism. It didn't matter if I was writing. What difference would it make in this crazy world? Michelle was fast becoming the center of my world and perhaps Bob saw this. Maybe he could see how this woman's short afro, beautiful eyes, body, laughter, walk had conquered me. If this was colonialism, then I never wanted to be independent. Why have my own flag, control my economy, when an afternoon making love with Michelle was why kings walked away from kingdoms and poets embraced silence. What was there to say after love? But I told Bob I was still writing and he told me to pull out a piece of paper and write down the following names: Sonia Sanchez, Marion Brown, Askia Muhammad Toure, Ebon, Carolyn Rodgers . . . at All Soul's Church.

The program was held a few days after our meeting on campus. I went to my first reading with Michelle. I arrived early and was very nervous. Bob selected me to be the first reader. Several hundred people were in the church. I dug in behind the podium like a young Jackie Robinson. I knew there were many young writers better than me. The city was the home of Gaston Neal and Adesanya Alakoye. But I was Jackie from Howard, a good clean kid from the South Bronx. My brother had been a monk, my father worked in the post office, my mother in the garment industry, and my sister was a nurse. I leaned into the mike, gripping my first poem, a short piece about Negroes being afraid of the revolution. The words left my mouth and were smacked across the room with applause. Wow . . . a single in my first at bat. The evening was young and I was young. I stepped off base after the first poem and thought about stealing second and perhaps making writing my career.

IV

*N*o one in our family had any idea what kind of foolishness my brother was getting into in Washington. When I saw him it was usually at Thanksgiving. He always brought home a girl from Howard with him. I remember a cute one by the name of Sue. She sat in the living room talking to my mother. Everything my mother asked her received the same response, "Yes, Mrs. Miller." I'm certain that girl was as high as a kite or anything else that was flying into LaGuardia Airport. What a light she had in her eyes; you could see into the dark with them. I was working with drug addicts and knew all the symptoms. Now, when Gene came home with this child Michelle from Chicago, whew, I knew he was shooting up or maybe just making love in his dorm all day and never going to class. The girl was fine and fast. My brother's nose was open so wide it had four lanes. I told my mother this was going to happen. No sex when you're young can lead to a serious addiction later in life. I know, I work around sick people for a living.

V

Bob Stokes waited until after my graduation before taking over my education. He provided me with instructions on how to become a writer. There was not much he could do with me while I attended Howard.

In 1970, I majored in Afro-American studies and read more black books than ever before. I became familiar with poets like Sterling Brown, whom I would hear reading on campus now and then. The critic Stephen Henderson arrived from Atlanta along with a number of new black professors. James Cheek assumed the presidency of Howard from James Nabrit following the student protest. Kent State and Jackson State changed the lives of young people around the country. Still, one could have a serious panty raid attack against the Women's Quadrangle or sit on the Wall on Fourth Street and wait for openings into the black middle class.

In Cook Hall, in rooms next to mine, the McKay twins were still confusing folks about their identity. Tim from Savannah had discovered some unknown secret that would make his girlfriend moan and holler during the hours of coed visitation. Once Michelle and I banged on the wall and told her we knew she was faking . . . it couldn't be that good. In the midst of so much lovemaking and blackness, I entered the seventies without any sense of who I was or who I was becoming.

Many times I thought about the difference between going to class and going to the cafeteria. A person has no idea what they want to eat; they just know they are hungry and must select what's behind the glass. You look at what you can identify, what other people are eating, or you simply pray you won't get sick. This is how I was beginning to approach each semester. I moved from being a history major to Afro-American studies. It was a new department, created only because of the student protest back in 1968. The classes they offered would further baptize me in the religion of black consciousness. Many of the teachers in the department would later become good friends. This was important for the Bronx Bomber, the newly defined E. Ethelbert Miller.

I had a few poems but was far from deciding that I would become a writer. Many years ago I thought about following my brother in his monk footsteps. A life of contemplation, of pursuing goodness, developing one's inner self, taking a vow of silence, fasting, forgetting about the flesh and its temptations. Friends like Reggie had started to read books by Krishnamurti, and the Holy Qur'an. A few students in the dorm burned incense for spiritual reasons, not to cover up the popular pot smoking.

Sunni Muslims from a local community mosque started giving us pamphlets and telling us about the Islamic faith and how it could change our lives. Being black was only part of the equation. A Howard education provided me with a job after graduation but it could not provide me with the tools and equipment for living. What pulled my brother toward the path when he was young? How do you decide what to do with your life. Surrounding me are black men and women who want to be doctors, lawyers, and dentists. I contemplate the life of being a lawyer and maybe going into politics. But not for long. My defeat by Charlie Goodman for sophomore class president ended my fascination with running for office, and it seemed as if I embraced poetry and art like someone taking the train down to Greenwich Village looking for a café where one could sit and discuss Camus and the latest recordings by Sonny Rollins or maybe Ornette Coleman.

If life was simple, we would all be farmers or maybe

musicians holding a trumpet or saxophone to our mouths. But what music would we play? What song? Whose band is this anyway? I enroll in two classes being offered by the Afro-American Studies Department; "Blues, Soul and Black Identity" and "The Black Aesthetic." Both were taught by Dr. Stephen Henderson, a small man with thick glasses, very intellectual, quiet, and a lover of the blues. I know nothing about who he is. I just need to take more classes in order to graduate.

How do you meet your father when you are born? It's not like coming out of your mother's womb and looking back at her and saying thank you. Who is this guy someone hands you to? A father? What is his connection to your new life? Where was he for nine months? Missing? So here is this new Professor Henderson on campus, walking into my life at this time, fathering words and ideas, telling me about the Black Arts movement and what black poetry is and should be. Where would Michael Jordan be if he was still coached by Doug Collins? What if Phil Jackson didn't believe in Zen. So many of us would never find our game. It would be lost on playgrounds and campuses, or trapped in the post office or bank.

Sometimes you reach the station and you have this ticket for your destination, but there are two trains running. Which one do you take?

CHAPTER EIGHT

I

I walk into one of Henderson's classes. It's being held in the basement of Douglass Hall, where ROTC meets and the black conservative students who will one day put Ronald Reagan in office. Maybe this is the bowels of Howard. If I were Harrison Ford, I could snatch something out of one of these rooms, escape, and have the entire black race chasing me. Maybe in my bag there would be the true secrets of how Kwanzaa was created, who killed King, shot Malcolm, and told the Egyptians the pyramids were on loan from Saturn. I take a seat next to Susann Thomas. I soon discover that she collects elephants. Pictures and sculptures of elephants. Cards and jewelry with elephants. Susann, Susann, another woman stopping me in the middle of myself, of who I am trying to become. Susann, Susann, another woman leaving the station with my heart. I open my book and listen to Henderson talking about the blues. Yeah, it ain't nothing but a good woman on your mind.

II

I met Susann in 1994, She came to Ethelbert's reading at the Ninety-second Street Y. It was a special reading for his book *In Search of Color Everywhere*. We spent the entire evening laughing and talking like sisters. I discovered Susann lived a few blocks from my mother, and would even talk with her on the telephone. That was something I knew made this woman special. If my mother called her on the telephone, then this girl was family. How come I am only meeting her now? Who is she? My brother is a person carrying a load of secrets. Every time I read one of his books I learn something new about him. So he calls her Susann, Susann. They had to be lovers at least once. Girlfriend has too many poems written for her. But then they seem to be too much like brother and sister, the way Richard and I were before Monkey Gene arrived. I think of all the memories from Longwood Avenue. So much is gone. Richard. My father. If I wrote my story then you would know the meaning of the blues.

III

I keep taking classes until I think I have a college education. The good news is that I found a wife. Michelle and I decided to get married. She is making jewelry and has no idea of what she would like to do. She writes poetry. So it's the two of us now. Slowly, many of my friends are getting serious about their lives. Graduate school and law school and medical school are being discussed. It's like thinking about the NBA, or turning pro after being on the college team that tried to make it to the Final Four.

I sit in my room thinking about the future. Where is my dream? One night a poem comes to me. Words. Revelations. In the beginning I was a small boy standing on a corner in the Bronx waiting for my father. The sky is gray. I start praying. Suddenly words are escorting me across the street. I reach the otherside, proud of what I've done. I can write. My prayers are songs. I can make music. I can give color to the world. This is my life. This is my gift.

I wake, sweating, as if I've just made love to Michelle, but she is across campus in Truth Hall. There is a light in my room and I can see my future, who I would like to become. In a few years Bob Stokes will hand me book of poems by Henry Dumas. His words would become flesh.

Into the dawn light
the shadow walks behind you
Into the night
and it leads.

How do you explain to your parents that you wish to become a writer? Why is it so difficult to accept? OK. So I don't want to be a writer. I want to be a monk. I want to leave and be like Thomas Merton. Now . . . will you let me go?

IV

My father is very sick. It is late in my junior year at Howard. He has to have an operation on his lungs. The doctors are not certain what they will find when they open him up. I return to New York to join my family. At the hospital we all gather around my father, who is sitting in his bed laughing. He is trying to hold our spirits together. My mother rests her head on his chest. My father strokes her hair with his hand. This is one of the few moments of tenderness I will ever witness between my parents. I look into my mother's eyes and I realize her world has collapsed like a bridge during an earthquake. She is disoriented and cannot function. This is the first time I have seen her vulnerable and not in control. All these years I have seen my mother as the stronger one. I have always looked to my mother for guidance and support.

My mother is a small woman in a big hospital. Her children cannot comfort her. She looks at me as if I were a stranger. She calls for Richard and Marie. How many times in my life did my mother look at me and call Richard's name? How many times did she forget my name and then suddenly say . . . "Gene, you know who I mean."

It is obvious that I am not part of her world sometimes. This woman of secrets will never confide in her youngest child. Perhaps she believes she has given me away to a great aunt. Away from the hospital my sister assumes the position of power in the family. She tells me I better find a job when I go back to Howard. With my father not working and bills on the table at home, my education is a luxury. My sister suggests that I stop writing and focus on making money and helping out.

Richard is quiet during much of this discussion. Even at the hospital it was as if he was in the wrong room or maybe visiting the patient in the next bed. What was he thinking? My brother, the first born, my father's son.

Richard shouldn't be here. He should be somewhere in upstate New York, holding a rosary and saying his prayers. But here he is miles and years from his dreams, helping out, unaware that he will be the first to leave us. Or maybe he knew it all along and never told anyone, except maybe Carmen, who would be the last person to see him walking his dog.

V

The best thing I ever did at Howard was change my major to Afro-American studies. I remember the dean at the time trying to discourage me from submerging myself in what he saw as a fad. "What will you be able to do with black studies?" he asked me. I looked at my black hands and wondered if this was the comprehensive exam. Many "Negro" colleges were transformed by the Black Consciousness movement of the sixties. It was not easy, protests had to be held. The idea of creating a "black university" circulated among a number of black intellectuals.

When they created the Afro-American Studies Department at Howard with funding from the Ford Foundation in 1969, it was with the intention of creating one of the best departments in the country. Space was found for this new creation on the third floor of Founders Library, the main library of the school. Maybe this was the place Carl Van Vechten wanted to describe when he used the term "Nigger Heaven." The Afro-American Studies Department was located in a place you couldn't find unless you were lost in the library. Since the building was overheated and heat rises to the top, there was another environmental obstacle or middle passage to cross.

I was fortunate to secure a work-study job in the Afro-American Reading Room. This was the media and resource center created as part of the department. It was supervised by Raqib Esa, a practicing Muslim. Raqib was a slightly older gentleman and very devout when it came to his religion. Other Muslims on campus would often visit him throughout the day. I saw my first prayer rug hanging over a chair in the back of the room. While many of my dorm friends discussed the Islamic faith, Raqib was the first Muslim I met who actually said his prayers five times a day and also knew which direction to face when he said them.

Being in charge of the reading room and its acquisitions, Raqib selected numerous important texts on Islam. I started reading some of these books and engaging Raqib in discussions regarding his faith and lifestyle.

Working in the Afro-American Reading Room placed me closer to Dr. Stephen Henderson, the literary scholar, whose office was across the hall. We would talk on a daily basis. I would keep him informed about the new books on literature we had received. I also started to show him some of my poems. He offered praise, encouragement, and excellent criticism. He recommended essays and authors to read. Just hanging around Henderson was more fun than attending class.

Little did I know that prior to my graduation from Howard in 1972, meetings were being held to develop a new unit on campus. Plans were being made to form the Institute for the Arts and Humanites (IAH). This was the brainchild of Dr. Andrew Billingsley who was the vice president of Academic Affairs. The creation of IAH would change my life and have a significant influence on the development of black culture during the seventies and early eighties. Howard was about to enter another golden era and many people were not even aware of it. Henderson became the "reluctant" director of the new institute and surrounded himself with such writers as John O. Killens, Don L. Lee, and Clay Goss. A key adviser to Henderson was one of the founders of the Negritude movement, Leon Damas. The great poet Sterling A. Brown was called out of retirement to teach a class for the institute and appointed senior research adviser. I was selected by Henderson to be the junior research adviser.

There is an ongoing debate about what type of education blacks should pursue. Booker T. Washington once advocated vocational training. Thank God for his genius. One thing that I began to learn in my junior year at Howard was how to use video equipment. It was something I learned in the Afro-American Reading Room. With a camera and tape, I began to shoot whatever was black, moving, and of historical importance.

By coincidence, Steve Jones, who lived in my dorm, was a friend of Margaret Burroughs, an artist, writer, and founder of the DuSable Museum in Chicago. Burroughs was interested in getting some material from Sterling Brown. Since Jones was going to visit Brown at his home, I inquired about video taping the visit. Little did we know that Brown could tell a good yarn, and one reel of tape was not going to be enough. So by "accident" we started documenting the life of Sterling Brown. Stephen Henderson immediately saw the importance of the work we were doing. He saw how vital it was to record and preserve information about African American writers. Prior to assuming the directorship of IAH, Henderson had a research grant that enabled him to bring a number of important writers to campus to be interviewed. What a wonderful part-time job I now had. I was taping programs for Henderson's research as well as meeting authors. Years later the poet Michael Harper would recognize and label me "Tiny's Man" a reference to me being Henderson's assistant.

If I didn't know then that there was a Black Arts movement taking place in America, I knew by the end of 1972. I was not only a young writer who was trying to write and find his voice, I was a person who had found something to believe in. The new faith was all around me, the disciples

71

many. I had been reading the poetry of Norman Jordan, Sonia Sanchez, Carolyn Rodgers, Nikki Giovanni, and, of course, Amiri Baraka.

One person whose "fingerprints" would be everywhere in the sixties and seventies was Amiri Baraka. I was still in awe after catching him read in the Burr Gym in 1969. Some folks claim he is the "father" of the Black Art movement. I don't know about that. I do recall clipping a picture of him out of *Ebony* magazine and showing it to my mother. "He looks just like Richard," she said. Mother to son or just another conspiracy theory?

VI

My brother's graduation from Howard was one awful hot day. Vernon Jordan was the commencement speaker, and when he shouted, "What do African Americans want?" I wanted to jump up and respond, "Some shade!" We were all sitting in the stands of the football field trying to protect ourselves from the morning sun. This was the day my mother had waited for. She had successfully put one child through college. She had ignored Gene's last-minute calls informing her he might not graduate because he had failed an economics course. No way. My mother was going to have her day in the sun. She had sewed too many rhinestones onto shirts and blouses to be denied.

On the steps of Cook Hall I watched my brother hand his diploma over to our mother. "It's done," was all she said. His comments sounded biblical, perhaps something from the Old Testament. OK . . . we've seen the miracle, now what?

CHAPTER NINE

I

Bob Stokes spoke to me before I graduated from Howard. He stopped me at almost the same spot as when he invited me to read at All Soul's Church. "Now your real education is about to begin." He laughed. Bob said this in a way that made me feel I had just wasted four years of my life. He was very happy I had taken classes from Stephen Henderson. These words would compliment the advice and information he would give me over the next few years. If my old friend Judy Howell wanted me to become involved in the community and move off campus, I was finally doing that. I found an apartment on Park Road near Fourteenth Street with my friend Roy McKay.

I left the dorms of Howard but not its campus. I decided to make the institution my literary base. My goal was to reach a point where the school's name was synonymous with my own. Was it Emerson who said an institution is only the lengthening shadow of one man?

A few months after graduation I married Michelle Calhoun. We went downtown and had a civil wedding ceremony, invited three friends as witnesses, ate some Chinese food, and took in a movie . . . the newly released *Superfly*.

It was almost another ordinary day until we rose the next morning and looked at each other. We were husband and wife. We were also living off campus in a small apartment near Sixteenth and P Street, northwest. The move out of the dorms and then away from Roy and other mutual friends was responsible for the first cracks in our relationship. Michelle had no idea what she wanted to do with her life. I was working full time in the Afro-American Reading Room at Howard. Nothing had really changed for me after graduation. Michelle and I were the type of young couple who should have decided to start robbing banks. Maybe find our faces on wanted posters in states like Wyoming and South Dakota. Somewhere in Cook Hall our lives lost their innocence. Home was now a place we were both responsible for. Even my idea of becoming a writer was in need of closer examination. Was I a desperado?

II

Raqib Esa got into a shouting match with a young man who wanted to borrow some books. I was in the back of the room and heard only part of their argument. It was unusual for Raqib to raise his voice, to see him now assume the old boxing stance of Miles Davis was shocking. Here was a man without a horn blowing hot air riffs into someone's face. When the argument ended, Raqib went to his desk and collapsed. He was embarrassed as well as tired. He looked at me and said, "Brother, I'm too old for this. Do you want this job?" So in 1973, I started working full time at Howard. My salary was paid for by the Afro-American Studies Department and the Institute for the Arts and Humanities. Was this a result of all praises due to Allah?

Like my father who worked in the post office and my brother who worked in a bank, I began the first of many years at the same job. Was I fortunate, lucky, or just afraid to move on to something else? I did enjoy my work in the Afro-American Reading Room. Every day was like Christmas with new books arriving. I ordered books and material that I hoped students would read. The reading room was a popular spot for student radicals. Many of the leaders of campus demonstrations climbed three flights of stairs to the top floor of the library to talk strategy and history. Many wanted to know about the good old days of 1968.

Nineteen seventy-three was a transition year for me. I was beginning to be known in Washington as a poet thanks to the work of Bob Stokes. He sponsored many of my early readings at a place called Dingane's Den on Eighteenth Street. I was always paired with well-known African American writers. This helped build my own audience as well as to establish a friendship with such poets as Jayne Cortez, Lance Jeffers, Askia Muhammad Toure, and Eugene Redmond. Some of the local poets didn't care too much for me. The jealousy and egos we often see in sports could also be found in the literary world. Who takes the last shot in a basketball game or who didn't get published in an anthology creates a similar distrust. Next time down the court you don't get the pass. So you soon become a shooter, a person only interested in their own career. You seek out people who can set screens for you. In the early seventies I saw all the players. A few deserve to be in the hall of fame while others should be benched for the rest of their lives. There are pretenders and many who will only make it to the neighborhood gym or open readings at the local library. Sometimes you are fortunate to meet gunslingers. A writer whose work is explosive and different. Writers with underground reputations come into town and change the aesthetics or start a new literary movement just by being seen in the same place twice. The gunslinger comes with stories and folklore.

The first time I heard about Ahmos Zu-Bolton was in the post office on Howard's campus. I had just opened my mailbox and taken out some letters. One was a rejection slip from the editor of *Hoo-Doo* magazine. By coincidence, my fellow poet and friend Amma Khalil was also in the post office and she had her own rejection slip from *Hoo-Doo*, also signed by its editor Ahmos Zu-Bolton. In her rejection note, he claimed he liked how she moved through the poem, but it was not *Hoo-Doo* poetry. "What's *Hoo-Doo* poetry?" Amma turned and asked me. I had no answer. Neither Bob Stokes or Stephen Henderson had ever mentioned the term.

The letters Amma and I received were sent from Louisiana. In a few weeks a man wearing coveralls walked into the Afro-American Reading Room seeking films to show at a community center in Maryland. He carried a bag of magazines or maybe it was just a pouch filled with goober dust, cat eyes, and rabbit feet. The man was southern in the way he walked, dressed, and spoke. If it were earlier in the century, it would be a perfect example of the Great Migration. Here was the type of guy Langston Hughes would meet while in high school in Cleveland, the guy who spoke in the rhythms poets wanted to capture on the page. Henderson had introduced me to the blues and African American folklore. Ahmos Zu-Bolton introduced me to himself.

III

While history might link your name to a place or another individual, it's comic books and movies that usually estab-

lishes your partner or sidekick. Or maybe it's best described by a line by Ntozake Shange about the Mississippi
meeting the Amazon. Ahmos and I were two different bodies of water. We were rivers flowing in opposite directions,
suddenly forced to occupy the same place in time. Maybe
Marx said the same thing about Engels or was it Nixon
talking about Kennedy?

IV

It might have been Susann who asked me why I got married, something she vowed she would never do. Why not
remain sane instead of driving someone crazy. Was it better
to be lonely inside a relationship? I was writing more and
needed more time for myself. I was beginning to understand the decision it took to begin one's journey. I was
curious as to how my brother could renounce everything
and pursue a simple life. Michelle was not my favorite nun.
One day in 1973, she woke up and decided it was time to
leave. Ahmos came by our Rhode Island Avenue apartment and helped me load her things into his van. She had
decided to move in with a girlfriend who lived in Southeast
Washington. I had hardly ever been to that part of town,
so saying good-by to my wife was like saying farewell to
someone leaving the country. Ahmos drove across the An-
acostia River and we both quietly composed poems in our
heads. He couldn't believe Michelle and I were separating.

Ahmos thought he would be first. His own marriage to
Kathy Zu-Bolton had become similar to one of those baseball games that go into extra innings. You reach a point
where you want someone to step forward and end it. Single, walk, home run, it doesn't matter how it's done. It was
funny how quickly Ahmos and I began running with each

other. From that first letter of rejection to his visit to the Afro-American Reading Room, we were working associates. I joined his staff at *Hoo-Doo* magazine, and Ahmos took my position at Howard working with the Institute for Arts and Humanities and joining me in operating the Afro-American Reading Room. All this had been set in motion when Raqib Esa decided to leave Howard and find a different Mecca.

V

Some nights I listened to Aretha Franklin and her voice would set me free. My marriage was not much better than my brother's. Maybe Richard was the smartest of all of us. Why not just love God? I became a Catholic a few years after Richard did. Was I running with the wrong crowd? My mother thought I had found a good West Indian man. All I know is that I got tired of being a woman watching cricket matches on the weekend. Yes, Aretha was my salvation, lifting me up when I had been knocked clear to the ground. Love is like a seesaw.

VI

In the closet of the Afro-American Reading Room was a sizable collection of jazz albums. As a student, I had contacted a number of record companies and requested donations. A few places replied with some gems. One day in March 1974, I went through the recordings looking for a good name to call a poetry reading I was organizing in

April. Jazz songs have some of the best titles. "Stella by Starlight," "A Night in Tunisia," "Lush Life," and "April in Paris."

In my junior year at Howard I named the Afro-American Studies Department magazine after John Coltrane's album *Transition*. So now I reached for *Ascension*. Yes, Trane was going where I wanted to go: the spiritual development in his last years, the pursuit of music as a way of talking to the Lord, as in "Dear Lord." Maybe Malcolm X was black manhood. John Coltrane was either our heart or soul, the goodness we needed to survive the madness of winter in America. I could listen to "A Love Supreme" all night long and maybe decide it was best to change my diet, my job, or my relationships. First would come acknowledgment, the resolution, and then pursuance. The goal was to reach that point of peacefulness and awareness . . . the psalm. The sacred song or poem. So difficult to do.

Ascension follows resurrection. I had read enough essays about the Black Arts Movement that I knew a new form of art was being created in the African American community. Artists were attempting to destroy the negative images that enslaved us and provide us with positive, uplifting ones. So after all this death and destruction, I felt one had to move to the next stage. I saw many of my fellow writers representing a new voice. Poetry should move beyond the rhetoric of revolution. Since Henderson was bringing many major African American writers to campus, I suggested the idea of an evening reading that would give local young writers an opportunity to shine and show their wares. Henderson agreed and even found funds to pay folks. The *Ascension* reading was held on a rainy April night in the Afro-American Reading Room. The room was packed with energy and talent. Poets from the campus as well as the community came to read their work. Little did

I know that this would be the first of well over a hundred *Ascension* poetry reading programs I would organize in the Washington area. How do you know when a movement begins? Fidel setting sail for Cuba with a handful of men, what was that about? No different from a roomful of poets. If someone was to say, "Hey, Stephanie Stokes went on to become editor of *Essence* magazine" that night, we would laugh and say, "Girl, just read your poem and sit down." Just the opportunity to stand in front of an audience and recite one's work is important for the person trying to become a writer. I felt I was providing the same outlet and opportunity that Bob Stokes had provided for me. So many of us wanted to publish books and there were few publishers. Letters from places like Broadside Press in Detroit came back with the backs of the stamps still wet from our tongues. So public reading was the key venue for getting work out. One could develop an audience and a demand for one's work by taking poetry to the people. What began on Howard's campus moved out into the Washington community and found a welcome at the Martin Luther King Jr. Library and the Folger Shakespeare Library. The poets who read on the *Ascension* series were not included in those Harold Bloom's catalogs. The work I was interested in promoting was aimed at restoring beauty to the world. Before I had sponsored enough programs to count on one hand, I organized an *Ascension* reading that featured a poet who changed my life.

Ahmos was driving his van, she was sitting in the back, we drove up Seventh Street and watched it become Georgia Avenue. From behind her sunglasses, I thought she was looking at the storefronts or maybe thinking about her upcoming reading. One never knows about poets. This time I knew no one was going to ask about the hours to the bookstore. The woman sitting in the back of Ahmos's van conveyed the type of coolness one associated with Miles Davis. When I saw her read, her lips were close to the microphone, soft words, blasting her political views, like Davis on his horn. A soft feedback, not enough to distract, and how could one be distracted from this woman who had it together.

Too often writers fall in love. They fall in love with words, poems, stories. Writers fall in love with the pictures of writers on books, on posters in bookstores, or when they sit down on a television show and talk to people who have never read their work. When writers fall in love, it takes place at conferences, on book tours, on college campuses, and in libraries. Suddenly the mail never stops and the telephone always rings. When writers fall in love with each other, it can be scandalous. No, they can't be together. Too different when it comes to style or genre. What about age? She's too young and he's too old.

I first saw this woman, or maybe I first saw her spirit, when I was in New York attending a book reception for the release of *Play Ebony Play Ivory* by Henry Dumas. Her beauty was a dream I tried to rise and wake from. I wanted to walk away but where would I go? It was 1974. Ahmos and I had taken the van on the road, heading north. It was his first time in New York. How far away were small towns in Mississippi and DeRidder, Louisiana?

Ahmos kept singing and laughing, his anger only coming to the top of his head as we got closer and the New York skyline emerged from behind the legs of New Jersey. "Why, can't you drive, fool?" he teased. "I can't look at the city and the road at the same time." Like sinners before us, and countless actors and musicians, dancers and singers we entered the city aware that we were new writers coming to pay our respect to the establishment. We were going to a New York City book party.

It was Toni Morrison who told us to fix the chairs, since we were early at the Random House affair. We were insulted, but we did as we were told. The evening was young and there was no reason for someone to give us a black eye and spoil our trip. The stars would come out and Ahmos and I would watch them enter the room: Melvin Van Peebles, Angela Davis, Nikki Giovanni and then there she was, the woman poet I had heard about, the woman whose work Stephen Henderson said was "heavy" language and saturated with blackness. She came into the room and Sun Ra was behind her. It was how he always opened a performance. The Sun Goddesses, beautiful women walking across the stage, showing the audience the way to Egypt and the next stop being Jupiter. Sun Ra coming behind, his genius a light for those who had ears. On this day Athena would appear again to help me on my journey, to give me the wisdom I would need to understand what it meant to be a writer. How lonely was the journey? How far did my father and brother travel before their stories and songs became too cumbersone and difficult to carry? Athena would disguise herself as she always does and so when I called across the room, this woman answered, "Yes, I am June Jordan," and she smiled and the way she tilted her head to one side said this is the way to paradise. And before I could say another word, Toni Morrison told everyone to be quiet and she began to talk. I never remembered a word she said, only how Loretta Dumas held her children against her body, knowing that their father was gone and no book could ever bring him back.

VII

Ahmos made a right and drove his van onto the Howard campus. He parked and I jumped out to open the back door to let June out. The softness of her hand touching mine for the first time. My mother a few years later would talk about older Jamaican women snatching up young boys. Maybe she was afraid they would escape the hands of someone like herself.

CHAPTER TEN

I

The first few years after graduation are when young people should go in search of themselves. They should find their path or what I call their bowl. The journey means confronting one's fears and finding their way out of no way.

I knew I wanted to become a writer in the early seventies. I had support from people like Stokes and Henderson. I was slowly beginning to know more writers living in the city. I did not have close friends my own age that I could talk to about books and writing. My brother, Richard, knew what I was going through. He too felt misunderstood, lonely, and often depressed, but he was living in New York and not close enough to put his arm around me. I was learning to write in loneliness not solitude. How do you write about something that is missing?

I compiled a few poems and published a chapbook titled *Andromeda*. The title was taken from a musical composition by Alice Coltrane. Many of the poems were short. There was nothing attractive about my first book. It was however a cornerstone, and I was slowly constructing myself. Being at Howard, working, meeting other writers, I felt I had something to share. What I became known for were love poems, and my verse had a softness that contrasted with the militant verse of my peers. Poets like Eugene Redmond talked about the need for African American poets to share the tender moments of their lives.

I could count my tender moments like they were a handful of pennies, slipping through my fingers. A few would fall to the ground and I would think about picking them up but saw them only as pennies; I could forget them and very little would change. My marriage to Michelle was something that slipped from my hands. One moment we were husband and wife living in a small apartment on Sixteenth Street, Northwest, and then near Fourteenth and Rhode Island Avenue, and then we were separating our record collections and arguing over who could have possession of "A Silent Way" by Miles Davis.

Love can be reduced to one song, a melody, something you remember from the wedding reception, or maybe whatever was the hit song when you fell in love. You hear it everywhere but especially at those moments when you are in bed and the lovemaking is over and outside a car stops for a red light. The radio is on and you hear your song and by the time you hum a few lines, the light has changed and the car is heading somewhere with the rest of your life caught in the refrain. Or maybe you are in a restaurant and the lull in conversation opens the door to a nearby room and the song is playing and you look into your lover's eyes and nothing is spoken because the song says everything and you remember the first time you heard it. The memories are what you cling to and not even those can make you stay when you know it's over.

When Michelle left, I made a promise to myself that I would never place a woman before my work. I was learning that a woman could enter and exit my life but only I could turn my back on my poetry and muse. Maybe I was slowly becoming a writer or simply a man learning the ropes of life while trying to jab his way into knowledge.

II

I liked Mickey. She was pretty and funny and filled with life. I was happy to see my baby brother married. We could never get Richard to date. His close friends were always men and so maybe he wasn't interested in women. He had little patience with people, and he hated to hear me laugh. He said my voice was too loud for his ears. Now Daddy, he loved Mickey. He thought she was beyond beautiful. Maybe Mickey brought back those Harlem memories, those sweet dandies that Langston wrote about. I don't know. There was that unfortunate incident I recall when my mother asked Mickey to set the table for dinner and the poor girl didn't know where all the forks and spoons went. Mickey was the first non–West Indian to find a place at our table. My mother had a way of making you feel bad that was unforgettable.

III

In the early seventies, those years after graduation, I saw my father only a few times a year. Washington was as far away as Paris or Istanbul. I seldom wrote to my father and his dislike for talking on the telephone made it seem as if we were experiencing frontier living. The bride had arrived from Chicago and I was now trying to keep the fences up. Maybe I was an outlaw, trying to survive despite everyone's belief that I had wasted my college education. On those occasions when I did return to New York my parents would ask about school. Since I was still at Howard, they figured I was in school. Was my graduation a secret? They did attend, didn't they? Had my life as a writer become a secret kept from the other members of the family? Aunts, uncles, and cousins? It didn't make sense but the secrets of my family would never make sense. Clues began to appear with the death of my Aunt Winnie. At her funeral in 1975, a second son walked up to the casket and left tears enough for two. My brother, sister, and I would learn that our new cousin had been given away at birth to be raised by someone living on Long Island.

Was this not proof of what could have happened to me? I remember the rumors that are now suppressed and described as foolishness or something I made up. My mother found a new path from the bedroom to the kitchen, one of avoidance and something I guessed made her a sleepwalker. Maybe she was the last witness of the "vanishing son" who was taken from a home in Brooklyn. Since she was the oldest of three girls maybe it was her responsibility to prepare the child for his new home. How much guilt could grow out of scars this deep? Best to just block it out like it never happened. The years passed and the child returns bringing his own memories. What a strange coincidence that the "lost" son, Aunt Winnie's child, found a place to live in the building next to my mother in lower Manhattan.

My father said nothing after Aunt Winnie died. Another death to him was like the mail he sorted. It had to go somewhere. That's what happens to every life. It has to go somewhere. Very few deaths in my family would bring me back to New York. I was now finding my way; words and poems were opening doors to a new world and identity. I had buried Eugene Miller without ritual or prayer and was becoming E. Ethelbert Miller, the poet.

IV

The writer's journey is a discovery of geography as well as spirit. In 1972, I went to the USSR, and followed this expedition with visits to Tanzania in 1974 and Cuba in 1976. These trips changed my consciousness like a young LeRoi Jones stumbling through Cuba after the revolution of 1959 and writing the first section of *Home*. By the time I was in my twenties I had traveled farther than my father had ever gone. Our lives were so different. I was embracing words while he was confined to silence. My mother hinted that he was impressed by the many places I was fortunate to visit. I could never bring him back anything. My father rejected most material things. The few items he cherished, like a piano or guitar, were things he polished until they shined and one knew better not to ever touch them. These things belonged to God, and like foolish children my brother, sister, and I saw his wrath. Marie once had a saucer thrown at her head. I was always told by my mother to wait until my father got home if I did something beyond what she considered her control. Under the bed was the best place to hide, for if my father was tired he was not going to bend over to look into the dark.

Many of my trips were adventures into darkness. I never knew what to expect. I did know that I disliked traveling with groups. On several of my trips overseas I was always with people who would define themselves as progressives. They were easily duped by guides. My politics in the early seventies placed me on the Left. However, having touched the fabric of prayer rugs in the Muslim community, it was almost impossible for me to become a true believer in a secular socialist camp. I was motivated less by ideology and more by my parents values. My mother respected people to the point of changing her voice and accent when speaking on the telephone. She was often concerned with what people would think, and so my shoes had to be polished, my hair combed, my ears cleaned, my shirt ironed, and no lint on my sweaters or pants.

No wonder my brother converted to Catholicism. Where else could Richard go? How far away was he from becoming a Trappist monk if he was around a father who seldom spoke? It was easy to take a vow of silence. My mother, with her secrets, was also a model for a faith that recommended confessions. So my travels took me away from New York and Washington but closer to the place where souls live.

V

The early 1970s was a golden era for Howard University. The National Afro-American Writers Conferences and the many activities of the Institute for the Arts and Humanities, under the leadership of Stephen Henderson, established a cultural Mecca if not a place for baptism into blackness. With writers like John Killens, Haki Madhubuti, Leon Damas, Sterling Brown, and others around, the place had more writers than bookstores in the area. Killens was good at organizing conferences and bringing people together, even if many were simply his old friends from the Harlem Writers Guild in New York. This was my introduction into literary politics and would help to explain the cultural developments in cities like New York, Chicago, and Atlanta.

Every literary conference is organized around a person-ality. Ahmos Zu-Bolton and I had to fight to invite writers who were outside the "sphere" of Killens and Madhubuti. We pushed to invite Ishmael Reed, Ntozake Shange, and one year the lesbian critic Barbara Smith. All in all a number of good presentations were held. The National Afro-American Writers Conferences helped to document the Black Arts movement, thanks to Harold Burke who was hired by Henderson to record things on audio and video tapes. It is unfortunate that the taped recordings are now located on the Howard campus gathering dust or maybe they have disappeared like the Oscar won by a famous black movie actress. So many things now . . . gone with the wind.

V1

My separation from Michelle was followed by a series of relationships that are best now forgotten. Almost all of my collections of poems are filled with desire that would haunt me into the 1980s. It would reach the tumbling level when I met a divorced photographer named Sandra. Maybe my soul was indeed taken, as she photographed me on a reg-ular basis. I met her at the Watha T. Daniel Library. Sev-eral friends were putting up a literary exhibit on the negritude poets, one that would honor Leon Damas. Folks were hanging large posters, talking and rushing to com-plete the work that should have been done a few days earlier.

I was never one for looking over my shoulder at a woman or going up to an attractive person and asking her to dance or even stopping her in the street. They would stop me first, the way Michelle had done. But now as a poster falls off the wall I watch Sandra bend over to pick it up, and my eyes are without a camera to record what I see. Did I fall for a woman's butt in tight pants? Or was this a divine sign that I would misread and all the punishment reserved for sinners would be my inheritance? Why was I attracted to photographers? Didn't June own a camera? I can't recall and this is what makes this so difficult to write.

We are on Sheridan Street and she parks her small car. How much of my life will be spent on this block? If I ever had sexual fantasies, they would be amateur recordings of what I experienced on this northwest street in a quiet neighborhood. Once I walked from my apartment, up Sixteenth Street, in a snowstorm, because the loving was so good. Little did I know that I could have been Bigger Thomas out on the same night, fighting the same white snow, and not know my life would be changed, not by murder, but by a woman who used sex like a drug. I was addicted and for this I would discover the blues, the painful hurt of being left at the station, or listening to the telephone ringing with no one to answer my call. Yeah, the blues waking me up one morning.

When Sandra one day out of the blue said she didn't want to see me again, the poems came quick from a place known as anger and hurt. I discovered that loneliness was a sword that had cut too deeply. Before all the books about girlfriends and waiting to exhale, a woman had taken my soul and not even given me a blanket for comfort. I was left in the middle of an emotional sea with no coastline in sight. If a ritual had been played out, I was now ash, a black body smoldering and no longer able to see the light of my self. If ever I was lost, it was now. I called and called, weeping and showing all the withdrawal symptoms of an addict. I knew it was the sex and not the love, just as I knew the difference between photographs and negatives.

I was in the dark and the darkness would engulf me and I would forget about the goodness I had wanted to pursue. Bob Stokes had met her once and had simply shook his head and said, ". . . watch it, boy." So one looks across the landscape and wonders where the buffalo have gone.

CHAPTER ELEVEN

I

Despite my battles with loneliness and moods of depression I was able to put together an extensive network of literary contacts in the seventies and eighties, consisting of writers, agents, publishers, editors, critics, publicists, newspaper reporters, filmmakers, musicians, artists, scholars, librarians, radio talk show hosts, unknowns, little knowns, celebrities, and old girlfriends. It had started while in college and being around friends enrolled in fine arts who wanted to go to New York and Hollywood and see their names in lights. They wanted to reach the top of the mountain and look down from a height of fame. I decided the key to being a successful writer was working with as many people as possible, networking and staying in touch. I also realized the key to success was the control and access to information. Phone numbers, addresses, reviews, anything regarding writers and literature I attempted to gain access to or collect. Serving on a number of boards and working for literary organizations assisted in the gathering of this material.

My movement through the literary world was perhaps speeded up because of my race. I learned about the importance of federal funding of the arts from Ahmos and took my *Ascension* series into parts of Washington that were culturally segregated.

I was invited to join the boards of literary organizations, serve on panels coordinated by art agencies, and judge poetry contests in states like Utah. In many places I was the one African American in the room, a witness to the literary politics of America. I suspect similar situations occur for such writers as Henry Louis Gates Jr., Gerald Early, Charles Johnson, Toni Morrison, and others who move in the elite circles of the literary establishment.

The parties and meetings can bend your mind. You are guaranteed regular doses of insults and cocktail hours of invisibility in which you find a corner next to the other person of color who is serving the drinks. At meetings you can make a comment only to have the next item on the agenda discussed and your remarks completely ignored. It was stressful getting through three decades of literary activity. I am grateful to have made comrades like Liam Rector, Jeanie Kim, Peggy Shumaker, Dan Moldea, and Gigi Bradford. These are people who care about the arts and are willing to do something to protect them. They are also the type of people who will cover your back in a meeting.

Without literary institutions, writers would live a different type of existence. I learned this right after college and was fortunate to be around Ahmos Zu-Bolton. Despite his coveralls and his blues and country appearance, Ahmos knew a lot about how to get money from people. We were able to publish books and *Hoo-Doo* magazines under the business operations of Energy BlackSouth Press. Everything went well for a number of years until love laid Zu-Bolton down and he disappeared from Washington the same way he had appeared. I recall going by his apartment, knocking on the door, seeing a pile of mail, and thinking that if the Mississippi instead of the Potomac was nearby, his body might be floating in it. Maybe it was haints and stuff the old folks tell you to leave alone—but being from the city, I didn't know what to do. Prayer is for people who need it and I think Ahmos needed it more then me. After two months he called from down South, his voice sounding like it had a woman in bed next to his body. We spoke for a few minutes, but things were never the same between us, the river overflowing, washing away the banks of friendship.

II

If Ahmos was a conjurer and his poetry had all the richness of a Henry Dumas, then it was his stories that whirled around my head and gave me an appreciation for the South. My roots could be traced to an island in the Caribbean or maybe just the island that was my father's life. The writer's life offered no comfort or boat. I could sail back by memory into oceans of feelings and incidents, but then what? I had seen my brother drown from a broken heart. I had been shipwrecked by a divorce from Michelle and knew that June was more myth than woman, goddess instead of flesh; and Sandra with her camera was an executioner who had given me cold beer and a bed on many occasions, and I could have ascended into heaven one night after sex. . . .

Yes, prayer is for people who need it. If you don't pray and think you can solve things on your own then you'd better be able to understand omens. In the middle of the eighties a young poet came to my office with a chapbook of poems. The title was *Black Rose*. The work was not challenging, but the writer was pleasant and our conversation

97

in the newly renamed African American Resource Center was filled with moments of laughter. A week later, as if I had seen John the Baptist, another woman, dark skin, short afro, and attractive, came by my office with her poem "Black Rose." I was struck by the similarity of the two poems I had read in such a short span of time. This second one was composed by Denise King, a woman from Iowa. If one had to select a state where you would meet a black person who would influence your life in a big way . . . Iowa was not one of the states high on the list. You say "Iowa" and think about the state and wonder what type of people would live there. What great migration left a family stranded in a field outside the South and not close enough to the North or a dream? Denise was from a family in which her parents named their three daughters, Deborah, Diana, and Denise. Like something out of Shakespeare you could try to make sense out of Denise's background and still fail.

Was I looking for a second wife? No, not this time. I was writing and building a literary reputation. Michelle had taken my record collection and maybe that's what I found interesting about Denise when I entered her Maryland apartment for the first time. Here was a black woman without a record collection or record player. How did she breathe? Maybe this was a clue I overlooked. The absence of music in a woman's life, no jazz or blues, just what could a man hum in her presence?

It was one visit, one meal, and a night of love, and Denise and I were a couple living together near Fourteenth and Rhode Island in a place called Newport West. How could I ever explain this to my mother? But I did. I called her one evening and told her I had met a woman who was special and different. My mother changed the subject and asked about the weather. All I could tell her was that it was dark outside, Black Rose standing in my room.

III

I don't remember all the names of the women who lived with him. When I separated from my husband, I had to leave New York. I called my baby brother and told him I was coming to Washington for a few days, maybe to look for a new job. He had that cute duplex apartment; you walked in and walked up the stairs to the living room and then you walked up a second flight of stairs to the bedroom. I thought that was nice. He had all those books, everywhere, and the cats, just like Richard. I spent the first day just answering the phone, trying to spell all the African names of people who called. One was Niama, so sweet and a nurse just like me. I woke early one morning and found her and my brother curled up together on the couch. All the pictures from my wedding were cut into little pieces before my husband went out the door; we never slept like that during all the years we were married. I turned and went back into my room, closing the door to everything and what was left of my life.

IV

Maybe around 1980, I thought about Jimmy Baldwin more. We would read together at the Howard University law school and he signed my copy of *Time* magazine, the one from the early sixties when he was on the cover. Like Baldwin, I selected to live in exile away from the South Bronx and New York like it was Paris or Istanbul. Washington was my home by the river. Why didn't I spend more time by the Potomac, staring into the northern arms of Virginia? I never cultivated the style of a poet. My clothes and mannerisms never changed to the point of making a statement. Some of my friends worked hard at being writers. Their dress, and reading habits placed them on a corner outside a café in Greenwich Village.

Denise made me tougher. Like Bundini coaching Ali, she made me stand up and speak out more. She stopped writing her own poetry. Her own words connected with mine.

V

There is a moment when you feel it . . . the rush that comes after you've written what you know is a good poem. Or maybe it occurs in the middle of your voice while you're reciting a poem in front of an audience that is listening to your every comma and period . . . every breath. Some folks never make it there. They stop for some reason. Time, talent, or just the tears it takes to get where you want to be. It would take a number of published books before I felt I had arrived as a writer. The book. That's what so many writers want. The feel of the cover and pages, one's name on a bookcover, a book on a shelf, in a library or bookstore. The book you give to your mother and father and all the cousins you no longer see. The book in your hand or bag. So many of us counting the days until the book arrives. It comes and you hold the box or envelope like you were getting ready to give someone an Oscar. You have that first copy of your book in your hands, and it affirms who you are and all the things you've been doing for months and years. In your hands, it's not about words but the touch, the feel, the smoothness, the smell of the paper, and the pleasure it gives. You flip and skim the pages, looking to see if everything is there. Later you will find a misspelled word, a missing punctuation mark, but for now the book glows and you wish to share this feeling with someone, anyone.

But who do you call? So many times I've just placed my new collection of poems back into the envelope and forgotten about it. Who could I call and inform about my new book? Who would become excited and want to celebrate?

VI

Revision. How often do you revise a poem? The question is asked in workshops and interviews. I tell people I write fast; I revise when I prepare to send work out for publication. It's not a big problem or an enormous task. Revision is like divorce or separation. Changes. How different is the second draft from the first?

CHAPTER TWELVE

I

The idea of getting divorced, and then getting married again was strange. Denise and I lived together as the 1980s unfolded. Republicans and black conservatives came to town. Jelly beans were given out along with cheese, and the homeless became more visible. The golden era at Howard was over. The right wing virus would affect even the blackest institutions. I watched as I entered my thirties. I was the baby of my family, trying to grow a beard like one of those revolutionaries that followed Che. Was I out of step with the times? Was the goal of becoming a successful writer still beyond my reach?

Denise and I went to Barbados in 1980 for my thirtieth birthday. It was a spiritual journey and a turning point in my life. In many ways I was looking for family and clues to that West Indian connection. We rented a small vehicle and drove around the small island. It was one of the few times we traveled together. We did all the things tourists do. One afternoon we had lunch with the writer and editor John Wickham.

I was fortunate to know a number of important Caribbean writers like Wickham. The most impressive was

C. L. R. James. James had taught at Howard in the early seventies. His class on Pan-Africanism was a popular course. Drum and Spear Press had published *A History of the Pan-African Revolt* and the rumor circulated that one of the most important books after maybe *The Wretched of the Earth* by Frantz Fanon was *The Black Jacobins* by C. L. R. James. When C. L. R. lived in Washington, he resided on Sixteenth Street in one of those large apartments buildings where it seemed as though everyone had a mistress, or perhaps a good view of the city. James had young people taking care of him. He was a tall, handsome man. His lanky frame was usually found in bed surrounded by books and the television playing afternoon soap operas. Here was a man who was a contemporary of Trotsky, a friend of Kwame Nkrumah, George Pademore, and Paul Robeson. He was one of the most brilliant men I have ever met. His mind worked constantly and missed no shadows. James was always asking questions and more questions.

Sometimes I would bring him books written by African American women writers. He loved Ntozake Shange, and felt her work was important to the African American community. James read everything. The last time I saw him alive was in England in a small apartment in London. He lectured to me about the cultural importance of Michael Jackson and Fred Astaire.

If I could live as long as C. L. R. and be a witness to history, perhaps the idea of writing poetry would have even greater meaning. By 1980, I had reached the level in my career at which old friends stopped asking if I was still writing. They knew this was not a hobby. I was still running the African American Resource Center at Howard and the position kept me in touch with an entire directory of graduates. Giving poetry readings across the country also kept me in contact with old faces. Yet some encounters took place where one could sense the subtle measure of ego as a business card was pulled from a wallet or purse. "So, what are you doing, Ethelbert?"

Slowly I pull my wallet from my back pocket like a martial arts expert. I keep a rubber band around it. How many African American men walk around with rubber bands around their wallets? My father did it, and it seems as if I remember countless men in barbershops reaching into back pockets, pulling those wallets out held together by rubber bands. Wallets that contained more paper then money. Small slips of paper stuck between pictures and receipts from a grocery store. When I was about ten or eleven, my father came home late one night and told my mother how a woman had tried to pick his pocket on the subway, but the rubber band on his wallet got caught on the button of his pants. I pull a business card from my wallet. The card, like in the old television show *Have Gun—Will Travel,* I take care in the design of my card. I always have. I need something that can change a conversation. I present my card. My business is poetry.

II

*F*or a long time I didn't want to think about the West Indies or even hear a West Indian accent. When my husband left me I closed my ears. I decided to be my own island. No more men first and me second. I saw myself becoming too much like my mother, spending an entire life in a kitchen cooking for a man. Relationships are too much work. I don't know how my brother does it. I would rather operate my heart like my own private business.

III

How do you measure success as a writer? Is it the number of published books? The number of awards? One's personal satisfaction? Levels and degrees of measurement? In 1982, things began to happen for me. It was as if I were a baseball team that made a trade during the off season and finally snagged a free agent. A player who could take everyone to the playoffs and maybe the World Series. The fans in Washington were beginning to take notice of my presence. It was a city in which the poet Sterling A. Brown was Babe Ruth.

Mention Washington, D.C., or Howard University and the name Sterling was one that had been shinning for ages. Around Brown was a cult of admirers, consisting of students, radicals, and race men who remembered the old days. Any writer of importance would make the hajj over to his home in northeast Washington. Brown would entertain with stories and music. He was a genius, a gracious host with a lovely wife by the name of Daisy.

It was the small acts of generosity that made me want to be like Brown. It was great to be around him when he came out of retirement and appeared back on campus on a regular basis. He had an office in Founders Library around the corner from the African American Resource Center. He would often wander in and talk or ask about Stephen Henderson. Just a short conversation with Sterling Brown was a seminar in African American culture. It was like learning basketball from Michael Jordan. It would take me additional years to learn the fade away and no look pass.

I was on the panel that selected Brown to win the first Mayor's Art Award for Literature in 1981, and with the help of Grace Cavalieri and James Early we eventually succeeded in making him the poet laureate of Washington, D.C., before his death. I found it interesting that Brown had always been given an "unofficial" title of poet laureate but no official recognition. Once I was walking across the campus of Howard when a vice president of the university introduced me to a visitor as the poet-in-residence. I corrected him by stating that I was simply the person who picked up the mail for my department. I was a simple employee at the capstone of Negro education.

I knew my relationship with Howard would be one in which my service would never be recognized. I knew the history and the horror, the love affair between writers and schools that did not love them in return. This situation would be true for other writers I would meet over the years. Colleges and universities can be supportive of writers, or they can squeeze the last metaphor out of your blood, leaving you dry and angry going into middle age and early death. One can lose one's creative mind on a campus. At the same time the place can be the only space station in the galaxy. It was knowing people like Sterling Brown that convinced me Howard would be a good place to stay. When a person turns thirty, they should be able to tell which way the wind is blowing.

In 1982, I published my first sizable collection of poems, *Season of Hunger/Cry of Rain,* with Lotus Press. The company was founded and run by the poet Naomi Madgett. She operated it out of Detroit and it soon established a reputation as important as Dudley Randall's Broadside Press. Randall's company played a key role in publishing poets like Haki Madhubuti, Sonia Sanchez, and Nikki Giovanni. The Black Arts movement of the late 1960s had been dependent on the building of institutions like Broadside Press.

Finding a publisher is always difficult. Without word

of mouth and friendships, many writers would be naked, with nothing, no book, nothing. My small chapbook *Migrant Worker*, published in 1978 by the Washington Writers Publishing House, received help and support from poet and radio host Grace Cavalieri. Things were no different with Lotus. Naomi Madgett was a friend of May Miller. I think May put in a good word for me. She was always doing something like that and she reminded me of that era I associated with Sterling Brown and Arthur P. Davis. The 1920s and 1940s. May possessed what I called black middle-class grace. A reminder to take your hat off when you came indoors.

June Jordan wrote the introduction to *Season of Hunger/ Cry of Rain*. Although she lived in New York, we constantly wrote to each other. For the cover design, the artist Mark Montgomery was generous with his time and work. He was part of a talented group of artists one saw around the city in the late seventies. It included people like Greg Tate and Calvin Reid. These guys were so far ahead of the pack that if you were a musician you would swear your horn was broke before trying to play anything.

IV

How many writers, musicians, and artists have I met? I could stop here and list them. But how many are friends or just acquaintances? Each year it seems as if new faces replace old ones. There is unfortunately a large space around my heart that realizes the distance I have always kept between myself and other writers.

By 1982, I think, my mother slowly began to realize that I had become a writer and had developed an identity that was not food on her kitchen table. I was not pepper or paprika or salt. My brother however was stuck in a job at a bank and could not escape. On the weekends he played the organ at a church in Brooklyn. Marie had survived divorce the way some African Americans survived slavery. The scars were on her back and the memories were always in the back of her eyes. She made it to work each day. As a nurse she observed others combating illness and accidents, and this reminded her spirit that the world is filled with darkness and light comes from candles and small acts of kindness.

How strange for me to move into a second marriage against the backdrop of the family I was born into slowly coming apart at the seams. Bad decisions and old age had become the inheritance of five people who had once shared meals on Longwood Avenue in the Bronx. My hunger to stay connected to my father and brother was often similar to a newly arrived immigrant walking down new streets looking into shops for familiar foods and smells. The world had changed and there was this growing sense of being alone that I could taste in my mouth.

Visiting New York was something I did less as I grew older. I had invented a new life in Washington and at times my mother would call me Ethelbert instead of Gene. Maybe this was her way of closing one door without opening another. One night, while talking to Richard on the telephone, he laughed and said, "Brother, you're so lucky to have escaped."

V

I was awarded the Mayor's Arts Award for Literature in 1982. It was one of those awards that's nice to receive but doesn't place food on your table. One significant contribution Mayor Marion Barry made to the city of Washington was to create a healthy climate for the flowering of the arts. He was a politician who understood the connection between politics and culture. One would have to cross the Atlantic and resurrect the African leader Amilcar Cabral to find another individual who understood the equation of literature, music, and art and how it connects to economics, food, and politics. The absence of art is poverty. As I was beginning to come of age as a writer, the national debate around the role of federal funding for the arts would begin to be an important issue. I would serve on a number of literature panels for the National Endowment for the Arts.

I never entertained the idea of just becoming a writer and writing a few poems and publishing a couple of books. To be a poet meant being a cultural worker or cultural ambassador. One embraced politics while advocating the importance of love and brotherhood. As a writer, the love of language was what made one come to the defense of public libraries that faced budget cuts. It was what took one into school classrooms, community centers, and prisons.

No one will listen unless you can develop an audience. A writer wins an award, appears on television or radio, or is quoted in a newspaper. All of a sudden they have that moment of fame Andy Warhol spoke of. I had told my mother that I wanted to be a successful writer by the time I was thirty-six years old. I wanted to have work in textbooks and find my name listed next to Langston Hughes and Pablo Neruda.

Too often a young writer will spend more time promoting themselves than writing. I have met a number of people who simply wanted to be famous. No poem, novel, or play, just fame. Every person who writes a poem is not a poet. A true poet is a person of the heart. Somewhere it's that thing called love that inspires one to sing. Out of pain, joy, and sorrow a man or woman can discover their wings.

VI

*W*hen I was a little girl I wanted to fly. Richard and I sat on the fire escape when we were kids. On nearby roofs, neighbors raised flocks of pigeons. I was collecting dolls then. What would I be when I became a woman? I gave myself three choices; teacher, wife, or nurse. One day I'm five and then I turn around and the middle of my life is about to begin with an apartment in Yonkers filled with plants and sculpture and a special shelf I started for my brother's books. Funny how he became this writer without telling anyone. How secretive he is. One or two months pass before he makes a telephone call. We don't talk much. When he comes up from Washington he visits Richard. I wonder what they talk about? Together they look like a pair of sad bookends. Both always talking about the future and upset with their friends or the jobs they are stuck in. I can't believe Gene is still walking around on Howard's campus. The boy can't let go. I thought the poetry was just a hobby but he's still doing it. When is he going to get a real job and earn some money? He has that old Greenwich Village look, and his clothes fit like the Vietnam War is still going on.

There are certain parts of New York where I refuse to drive. God, I hate Brooklyn. I feel like I'm in the islands with all the accents and people pushing their attitude into my face. When I was young I didn't mind the place. Now it just brings back memories I would prefer to just place in a flowerpot and sit on a window ledge. My godmother, Myra, lives in Brooklyn and I adore her. She was my mother's best friend in school. She is the type of older woman I could see in myself. So sweet, that's the taste she leaves in everyone's mouth. She came to this country from Barbados and made the promise to return before her eyes closed. Myra, a godmother. One needs a person in your life who is warm water. A person who becomes a place where you can relax, take your shoes off, soak your feet. If you never have that experience then you'll never know what home or friendship or love is.

I always wanted Richard to find a woman, but he didn't want the headaches and preferred the company of men. My godmother would talk to Richard when she saw him at family weddings and funerals. She could tell he was keeping something inside, a pain like a shoulder separation. Once I overheard my godmother talking with my mother. I was listening but she wasn't. Even my mother's best friend couldn't give her advice about her children. Now, here I am a woman in my late thirties wishing I had a dream to decorate or maybe a book to write. I need something of my own for these shelves.

CHAPTER THIRTEEN

I

Tell someone you're writing a memoir and the first thing they talk about is how young you are. I get tired of folks thinking I'm this young guy. Young people go off to war and never make it home. In the movies, they are the ones who open their wallets to show a picture of their new wife. You know as the wallet is passed around that the guy is going to be killed when the shooting starts. It's no different from Alex Haley knowing that Malcolm X would never hold his autobiography in his hands.

So why am I writing this? Why am I trying to recall what I was doing ten, twenty, and thirty years ago? Didn't Miles Davis refuse to look backward? I have a collection of dairies and notebooks in my home office. I have published articles and books on shelves, and I can walk across the room and step back into time and the language of old poems and love letters. This could be another slave narrative. I could be an abolitionist poet, a free person of color living somewhere near Boston. I could be a colored sailor recording my travels in secret as a boat takes me to another land.

Every journey has a purpose. This earthwalk I now take

is filled with the struggle to do good, to give testimony and bear witness for the people in my life. Here I stop to pause and count my blessings. I seek humility as much as success. I write in order to share wisdom with those who will follow me. I have learned fatherhood from my father and brotherhood from my brother. When I am tired and depressed, their souls refuse to rest. They say, "Ethelbert, rise and do battle in our name."

II

By 1984, the Black Arts movement was a cultural period to talk about as if it were the Harlem Renaissance. Many writers of that period were employed on college campuses teaching creative writing or African American literature classes; others struggled to keep food on the table, while a number fought the war against cancer and diabetes. A few reminded me of Jean Toomer and were mystical to the point of changing their diets and practicing safe sex.

I stayed in touch with many writers through my *Ascension* series. It was always good to be able to bring an exciting poet to Washington. I was raised by my parents to be polite, patient, kind, understanding, and the essential qualities necessary if you want to present poetry to an audience. Literary series can only last if they have financial backing or the atmosphere inside a space that is wholesome and suitable for artistic growth. The best place to read in Washington is the Folger Shakespeare Library. The theater is a nice size and the organization has always employed wonderful poetry coordinators like Jean Nordhaus, Gigi Bradford, Michael Collier, Saskia Hamilton, Liam Rector, and Aurelie Sheehan.

Visiting schools as well as prisons is something I began

to do more of as my career received wider recognition in the Washington area. I guess the desire to visit prisons was linked to my reading the work of Malcolm X, George Jackson, Eldridge Cleaver, and Etheridge Knight. With so many African American men behind bars, prisons seem more like off-campus housing. How slender the tightrope one walks. Lorton and Montgomery County Detention Center were places where my writing took me. How fortunate and vulnerable to be outside and free. Yet one is a witness to too many lives being destroyed. Did I escape my "burial" by having a father in my life?

III

It's not a matter of distance between us. My father lacks a vocabulary for love. He understands the language of life, which calls for him to provide and support his family. I could have been in the next room instead of Washington, D.C., and my relationship with my father would still have been the same. I mailed my books and articles about my work published in newspapers to my mother. Did she share them with my father or keep them secretly hidden in her dresser? On occasion, I called home and spoke with him on days when he answered the telephone. Our conversations lasted no longer than the time it took his key to open the front door when I was a child.

Richard and I grew closer because of the distance. I think he began to live his life through my accomplishments. He was proud of me in much the same way that a good athlete knows his younger brother is not only better than he is but perhaps might break a few records. Richard's life was over the minute he came out of the monastery. His heart was broken and not even the music he played on the organ or piano could heal it. He surrounded himself with books, African sculpture, plants, and animals. A trip to his apartment was often the best reason for visiting New York. If I saw him at our parent's house on Chambers Street, we could not talk. Our mother would prevent any conversation from taking place by pushing food in front of our faces and pacing back and forth, interrupting our words.

Marie was always working at the hospital in Yonkers watching someone bleed. Our family was never together the way we were back in the Bronx when we were young. The five of us, sitting around the dinner table, or going to the beach or Brooklyn. What a team we were. An African American working-class family. There is no picture of all of us together. If a photograph had been taken in the early 1980s it would resemble that of a Latin American family living under a dictatorship. Maybe one family member had "disappeared" or was killed because of politics. If our picture had been taken we would have posed in front of the piano. The piano is the instrument that connects our memories. Each one of us played at one time or another. We were all taught by Enid's friend Mrs. Walcott, who lived in Brooklyn in one of those brownstones owned by West Indians. In our family picture I would be found standing in the far back corner row. Enid and Egberto would be seated on the piano bench. Their eyes would be looking directly into the camera. The commitment they had to each other could be measured by how their shoulders touched. They would have a tired look in their eyes. A need for a vacation, maybe from each other. Those separate trips older couples make. My sister would be the beautiful one in the picture, standing in the other corner, her hair done in some attractive fashion of the day. She reminds one of a movie star whose name you've forgotten, but you remember her voice and the way her head turned when a man left her. My sister had to be photographed in black and white. Richard stands right behind his parents. One look at the picture and you know he is the one we all love, maybe too much. We are in the picture, surrounding him, suffocating him, preventing him from flying. Maybe my brother would be resting his hands on the shoulders of his parents. If this was a religious painting, he would be an angel. His wings would be open almost to the point of reaching the ceiling. Richard's eyes would be like the Mona Lisa's and his lips would be like hers. He would be smiling at the photographer and then the picture would be taken and his smile would be left on earth, a reminder of how the spirit can be seen.

IV

Did I ever really know my father? My brother? I wrote many poems about Chile, Nicaragua, and El Salvador. I wrote without seeing the landscape, the mountains, trees, and rivers. I used my imagination to create a place. Can you live with a person for a lifetime and never explore their personal geography? I tried to write about the two men in my life, but they wore masks.

V

My brother was always traveling somewhere. It was always to a dangerous place, a place where a war was going on or something. My mother and father were always worried. I remember that first trip he took in 1972. The boy had never traveled outside the United

States and the first place he goes is to Russia. Now what was over there? I could never see myself going anywhere unless I could work on my tan and put my feet in some warm water. Politics?

I could never tell what my brother was stepping into down in Washington. He must have been one of those Communists or Vietnam demonstrators. When he started listening to that Bob Dylan and Simon Garfunkel stuff in high school, I had to leave him alone. You can tell what a person is into by their music. Richard loved classical music. I was strictly soul: Sam Cooke, Percy Sledge, and Otis Redding.

I loved the music so much that I never felt the need to go anywhere. In my world everything could be found in a note or a beat. It's sad that both of my brothers couldn't dance. I had to hold the music to my chest all by myself. When Gene got married the second time, he and Denise walked down the aisle of that chapel at Howard as two musicians played "When a Man Loves a Woman" on piano and saxophone. I know Gene got that song from me. I never messed with politics. Maybe that's why I'm a nurse. I treat the body not the mind. What would I do running around in Russia or Cuba? Or that other place he went to in Central America?

My brother inherited the freedom that comes with having strange friends or no friends at all. I think I am a combination of my mother and father. They both keep to themselves. They are secretive to the point of always worrying. I think my mother is always looking over her shoulder. My father must have looked once and decided to never look again. There was nothing he wanted to remember after being left to himself even inside his own family. We all carry islands inside of us. I think that's why my marriage failed. It's also why my brothers were so close yet so far away. We were growing up together in the South Bronx and then suddenly we had our own separate lives.

I can see my brother living in Nicaragua, Chile, or Tanzania, and maybe sending greeting cards to everyone during the holidays. My mother would save the envelopes because of the stamps. She might place them on the piano in case someone dropped by to visit. I can see a relative from Brooklyn being impressed by the fact that Enid's children were seeing the world. If only we could have seen more of each other.

VI

I never had anyone to really talk to about writing. I never belonged to a workshop or group. Bob Stokes, Ahmos Zu-Bolton, Stephen Henderson were the people I perhaps shared a new poem with. In many ways I was swimming in the dark without a lifeguard. How many of us stumble into language, falling into this calling, which is more than a profession? I don't want this to happen to other African American writers. This is why I tried to establish creative writing programs at historically black colleges with the help of the Associated Writing Programs (AWP). How sad to find these institutions still in the nineteenth century failing to either document or preserve our literary history or refusing to teach it without coercion. There are many well-known African American writers who taught at Howard

University but were stuck teaching freshman composition classes or courses in African American literature. They were not teaching creative writing. So we failed to use the talents and skills of people like Clarence Major, Julia Fields, Julian Mayfield, Angela Jackson, and a bunch of others. Like Pat Riley trying to coach the New York Knicks into a championship, these schools have name recognition but don't know how to use all of their players. What can I say?

This writer's journey that I find myself on is also about service and helping to build institutions. I have respect and admiration for people like Haki Madhubuti and Paul Coates who are African American publishers, providing an outlet for dark voices and writers who would be silent behind an unknown veil.

CHAPTER FOURTEEN

I

I never had a writer's room, a place of my own. During my early thirties I walked around the streets of Washington with just a few dollars in my pocket. I was making a name for myself within the literary community. I was married and soon to be a father. It's funny how your life can change right in front of your eyes and you think you're watching a movie. I was at work when Denise called. She had gone to see her doctor because she wasn't feeling well. Now her voice had this joyful tone to it. She sounded like a person who had escaped jury duty, discovered a mistake the IRS made, or maybe had a winning lottery ticket hidden somewhere in the corner of her overcoat. "Guess what, Daddy?" She laughed over the phone. Her words bopped me upside my head like a beanball thrown by Nolan Ryan or Dwight Gooden in the old days. I was knocked down behind my desk like Don Zimmer. I was speechless like one of those early colored characters in the movies. *Feet don't fail me now*, I was thinking. How many times had I waited for a woman to say, "Well, don't worry, sometimes I'm late."

Denise and I had been living together so the news made us stop and look at each other again. I told her to drive from the hospital to Howard to pick me up. It was almost noon, so we decided to go to a restaurant on Eighteenth Street in Adams Morgan. We sat at a table facing the street, about to be new parents. What do you order? What is the first thing you want to place in your mouth after such news? Do you ask for just the appetizer, a drink, or just go to the main course? On the table in front of Denise and I was our love. A few months later we would be formally married in Rankin Chapel at Howard. We walked down the aisle together with two musicians playing "When a Man Loves a Woman" and this became our song. But right now we needed the silence for the moment to play itself. *This must be a movie,* I think to myself. I look at Denise and she has a glow, similar to the one I remember seeing after the first time I kissed her. Who am I? What small child will appear in a few months to call me daddy? How can I be a father when I am still trying to understand what a son or being a brother means? Who am I fathering? What soul will soon walk this earth, with a smile that resembles my own? Boy or girl? What name will we select? Do I have a taste for food? Love is such a full course. Denise is happy and this becomes a memory of what we refer to as the good days, the ones before distance would come between us like fog.

I began to share the news of Denise's pregnancy with family and friends. I can't remember anything my parents said. I know in the back of their minds they were thinking about the fact that Denise and I were not married. I could see my mother keeping the news from other relatives. What would they think? She might be the one at fault. My father said nothing. We never talked. In many ways he was like the veteran ballplayer who watches a new rookie arrive at the club. A player who is being called up from the minors to take the old star's place within the next year. Did my father see himself growing old? Did he think about those early days of his own marriage? The birth of Richard? Was he worried that I might have the same problems trying to earn a living, providing for a newborn? How was I to ever know. I was miles away living in Washington. My father disliked talking on the telephone and he never wrote a letter in his life. I was cut off from his feelings, his wisdom. What happened to the man-to-man talks? I needed a long walk with my father, but it was impossible to change who we had become.

Even Richard failed to be excited about the new change in my life. The coming of fatherhood perhaps reminded him of his own loneliness and lost dreams. It also meant that this would be an experience we could not share. We were brothers who loved each other, and now suddenly the title of uncle didn't fit upon his head like a crown. My brother was not the kind of man who would pat a nephew or niece on the head, give them special presents at holidays. He was more of the distant uncle type, the strange man whom other relatives talked about, the one who would leave you a large record collection after their death. Uncle Richard was not going to be the person you visited when you were home from college. Maybe you received a card with a few dollars in it upon graduation. By that time you just took the money and forgot to say thank you.

Who could I talk to about fatherhood? I had no close writer friends. My running buddy from college, Roy McKay, was one of the few people I shared my thoughts with. Roy had been working at a local television station for a number of years. Since he too had West Indian roots we laughed about all the bush tea we had in our system. Over a beer and lunch we often talked about our college years, exchanging gossip about who we saw from the old days. Roy was a survivor, a man who had no intention of getting

123

married. He was single, a homeowner in northwest Washington, the type of guy a woman would like to meet at a bar or someone's wedding. Being a twin, Roy could have someone else look in the mirror and take the blame for whatever he didn't want to feel responsible for. Roy had been a witness to who I had become since Cook Hall at Howard. I asked him to be my child's godfather. As the months passed, I watched Denise move into the final stages of pregnancy.

II

You place your hand over your woman's belly to feel your unborn child's kick. Maybe it's the middle of the night and your bodies rest like shells on sheets of sand. You hold each other as if you are afraid of the future, but welcome daybreak and the birth of new life.

III

I always wanted to have children, and when I couldn't, I couldn't find anyone to talk to about it. When I had my surgery, I slowly came to realize that I was the only person in that bed, room, and hospital. I was lying there looking at nothing and knowing that nothing would ever come out of me. I was holding on to being whole by a slender thread. I tried to talk to my husband about what I was going through, but he looked at me as if I had contracted a disease. His male mind just wanted to see himself in a small body. He wanted a little boy. Was that not the unspoken agreement at the altar when we took our vows? I was to be a mother by any means necessary.

Giving birth is the beginning of life and beauty. Sometimes I walk through the hospital where I work and I need to leave the emergency ward, so I take the elevator up to the floor where the babies are. Behind glass, or in arms, the newborns sleep, their eyes too new for this world. I like to inhale the joy and smell of motherhood, watching the first drops of breast milk falling into sheets and the space between us.

I am different from other women. I believed this for many years. When my mother called on the phone and whispered something about my brother in Washington living without rules, I wanted to join him. Who made the rule so that I couldn't have children? I cried many nights listening to my tears fall down the back steps of my heart.

IV

Denise's stomach is touching the steering wheel of our car. I worry about every sudden stop while she is driving. I pay more attention to detail now. It's like writing and finding the right word. Not a word taken from a thesaurus but from memory. I think about all the childbirths that end in miscarriages and the babies born with complications. I worry about how I will get Denise to the hospital. Where will I be? What if I'm giving a poetry reading somewhere? My entire approach to writing is changing now. I know it's also the key to taking care of my family. I will have to write more, push myself into new genres, perhaps even write a novel. There is a growing need to father words.

Fathering and birthing. How are they different? Similar? Denise has trouble walking up the stairs in our duplex apartment. Some nights she simply wants the child to be born. Is this like a writer's bloc, the failure to continue? In the early morning hours I push myself to write a poem. My work is still about the things outside: Nicaragua, South Africa, the social politics of the time. I don't know how to write about how my life is changing. There are no poems about fatherhood or waiting to hold a child. I do spend an awful long time thinking about names. What should we name this new person? How often does the poet complete the poem and leave it untitled. So what am I supposed to say to the nurse and doctor? Just call the baby, baby?

Naming ourselves is what many of us did in the late sixties. We took African names and Muslim names, and names we created like musical improvisations. So what if a child would be teased by other children throughout the eternity of adolescence. A name was hung around a child's neck and they either grew into it or found another name, a nickname given to them on the streets. If you were a boy on a basketball court, the game gave you your name. Your moves on the ground and in the air would find a rhyme coming from someone's mouth. A name might cling to you like lint if you embarrassed yourself. I remember a guy who lived on the eighteenth floor when I lived in the St. Mary's Projects. We were playing baseball and the guy couldn't play. No field, no hit, no nothing. He couldn't even run and he was just goofy and so Goofy became his name. One morning near the pipes in my living room, I heard his mother calling him, and then she calls him Goofy. The name stuck on his head like a bad haircut.

I think about naming my child after myself. Maybe by

the twenty-first century there would be an E. Ethelbert Miller IX and E. Ethelbert Miller X. How medieval and cool. Richard dug this idea. He was stuck in that old crusade period and had mastered Latin. He had watched the film *Becket* and had draped enough blankets over his head to proclaim himself king of the Bronx. Richard would change his name to Francis and then to Daud and when he died he would be called reverend father no different than someone calling themselves Maulana or Imamu.

The female persona has always been central to my work. In many poems I can easily adopt the perspective of a woman. So, if I have a daughter she will be called Jasmine-Simone. Denise loves the name Jasmine and my brother and I were Nina Simone fans. We loved her music and her attitude. Nina, dark and lovely. Sassy and outspoken. Nina is who you wanted a daughter to be like when you were not nearby to protect her. Jasmine-Simone. I love how it sounds. So musical to the ears.

V

"You better learn how to drive," my friend James Early tells me. I have as many ways of getting Denise to the hospital as Colin Powell had options during the Persian Gulf War. I know nothing about birthing babies, so I need as much help as possible. I talk to Robin Vázquez, a writer who lives near Thomas Circle. She has a car and is willing to help. I keep her number in my wallet like a talisman.

Where do poems come from? Midnight in April and Denise calls my name between contractions, saying, "Now's The Time." I help her down steps, into an elevator, to the curb, and pass the car door. Robin is here and we all drive into darkness. Late night when the streets are empty and maybe you can't catch a cab. Or maybe you're coming back from California or a trip to Atlanta and your plane lands at Dulles Airport. How far are you from home?

Denise is panting and blowing and all those birth classes are as helpful as a karate lesson when someone pulls a gun. At the hospital a nurse tells me to get ready if I want to be in the room when my child is born. I race into a nearby room to put on one of those gowns they give you in hospitals and your butt hangs out and you're not only embarrassed but cold too. Now I'm standing, watching a woman doctor bring life into the world. This is creation, like Miles putting his horn to his lips, Romare adding to a collage, Langston finding words for his dream. How do I feel? Parts of me are numb. Is this the *X-Files* where I am about to discover something no one ever told me about? Hey, Daddy, Daddy, welcome to the club!

VI

You hold your baby in your arms. Her eyes are closed. She has yet to see your face.

VII

April 21, 1982, and I am standing near the corner of Fourth and Bryant Streets, waiting for the G2 bus. Across town at George Washington Hospital is my firstborn child, Jasmine-Simone. It feels strange waiting for the bus, knowing or trying to know that you are a father for the first time. What does this mean? What do you do? Are you ready? The bus comes and I find a seat near the back, the place young kids go and pull the back window open. It's the place where one can talk loud or just sit and watch people enter and exit the bus as it snakes through the grayness of the streets, which are so much a part of me. Today, however, the sun is out and the smile on my face is something I didn't have to work on. I called my parents in the early morning hours and my father answered the phone, something he seldom did, claiming no one ever called for him. I was excited about my daughter's entrance into the world, and for a moment I could feel my father's breathing change like a runner pushing to make it to the next lap. I could tell he was happy but couldn't find the words, so he simply handed the telephone over to my mother.

Maybe it was sleep or the early morning hour that simply found my mother under a blanket, or maybe she was a runner far behind me suddenly realizing I wasn't going to be caught. I was a father and that meant I was no longer simply her child because I had a child of my own, someone she could not tell me to return. During the early morning hours, around the same time in April, she had given birth to Richard. My mother was forced to acknowledge that the world no longer revolved around her. I had created my own family and so I twisted the cord of the telephone and listened to the silence on the other end. My mother had nothing to say, and so I said good-bye and she probably went back to sleep and dreamed the entire conversation never took place. Maybe it didn't. I was left with an empty feeling. I took another coin, placed it in the slot and called Denise's parents.

What would have happened if I had become a father at an earlier age like so many other young African American men? Sometimes the bus is crowded and I look at the male faces and know that my life is no different from those around me. Was it the African writer Armah who said the beautiful ones are not yet born? I think about Jasmine, and how I stood tall in the hospital watching Denise give birth and the doctor holding my daughter up to the ceiling like we were all in an episode of *Roots*.

This morning, maybe around seven o'clock, I left the hospital and immediately ran into a friend whose name I can't recall, but it didn't matter because I would have told anyone who asked that I was a father, a daddy, and maybe I should have rushed home and written a poem. What I did instead was go back and clean the kitchen and prepare the house for my child. In many ways I felt like my mother looking over the sink, wondering who was making noise in the next room.

CHAPTER FIFTEEN

I

I am at the zoo, pushing a baby carriage. This is what my parents did. How many pictures of Richard, Marie, and me were taken at the Bronx Zoo? Was the rest of the world segregated? Were we too young to realize we were trapped? I head up the hill to where the Panda bears are. It's a cold day and Jasmine and I are wearing winter clothes. I should be taking a picture of her like my father. . . .

Being a father made me become very serious about my writing. It was no longer simply a means of self-expression, and artistic creativity; it was now also a tool with which I could provide for my family. A few weeks after Jasmine's birth I gave a poetry reading in northern Virginia. I got paid on the spot and came home with a car seat I had purchased with my small honorarium. I felt good that my writing was protecting me in this manner. The newspapers in the early 1980s were filled with companies downsizing and reducing their work force. I now went to sleep with one eye open. I would be foolish to believe a person's job could be safe at a black college like Howard. One factory was no different from another. It was impossible to follow the path of my father; no longer could one rely on working at one job and then retiring. I looked at the birth of my daughter as marking the change in my outlook on life. I was now responsible for the well-being of another human being. It was important to stay up late and write long into the early morning hours.

On September 25, 1982, Denise and I got married in Rankin Chapel on Howard's campus. Jacqueline Trescott wrote about the ceremony in *The Washington Post* the next day. What an event it was. Original. Very original. The marriage was combined with the blessing of Jasmine-Simone. Bernice Reagon, founder of Sweet Honey in The Rock, sang a song she had composed especially for the blessing ceremony. Fellow artists came from as far as South Dakota. June Jordan read a poem at the reception held at the historical home of Mary McLeod Bethune. Absent from everything was my brother. His depression was setting in and I knew it would be difficult for him to make the trip with other members of the family. Holes could be seen in our family fabric. I was discovering myself while my brother was measuring the size of his shadow. I stopped sending him my poems to read. We no longer shared books and music. For the next three years our conversations would be like cold coffee on a counter. I never knew about the changes he would make near the end of his life. He joined an obscure religious group that worked with the poor in New York. Richard's spirit was broken. He slowly gave away most of his possessions to friends. Much of his time was spent in libraries doing research and studying things related to the afterlife.

There were many times when I simply forgot about my brother. I was raising a child and my life as the little brother was over. How many of us reduce family relationships to telephone calls and holiday cards? Trying to get everyone together becomes possible only at funerals. A family becomes strangers and office partners, or the person next door who keeps your plants or feeds your cat when you have an emergency. Perhaps Richard started studying the afterlife in order to find a way to escape. A flight to another plane or level. How soon his departure would come, without warning.

II

The voices in my poems, where do they come from? How many times have I written something my mother once said. Her voice inside my head, raising me to assume a certain role. I should accept what is given. Be quiet, hush now, don't explain. My mother's voice so distinct and proper when a white person calls the house.

The phone rings in my office before the noonday break. I always just state my name, "Ethelbert." I let it hang in the air as if I were representing the homicide unit in a drug crazy city. On the other end of the line is my mother's voice, hysterical. "Gene, Gene, just bear with me. Gene," she cries. I recognize this voice. It is the voice of grief. It's blackness without a crack of light. It's pain and suffering. It's loss. It's emptiness and the hurt that won't go away. It's a sob in the far corner of the mouth and the redness of an eye that won't let another tear fall. My mother tells me my brother is dead. Dead the way you bleed before the blood flows. The world turns gray on this December day in 1985 and nothing matters anymore. I hang the phone up, pack my bag, find my coat, say good-bye to Mrs. Rose across the hall, and I leave the library, the campus, and walk across town to where I live on Fuller Street. It's the time of the day when not even the drug pushers are out. I enter my apartment, undress, climb into bed, and pull the covers over my head. What darkness will come and replace this day?

III

*W*hen the doorbell rings at my parents' house, I answer it. It's Gene, finally up from Washington. I hug him tight before he can even see anyone else. "It's just us," I cry. "Richard is gone; our brother is gone." I thought grief was like divorce. I thought it was something you just walked away from. How will I ever get over this? This is not another patient in the hospital, this is my brother Richard. Why? Who can explain this shit? God?

IV

My brother was the first person I helped to bury. I was responsible for selecting the coffin, planning the funeral service, and delivering the eulogy. I had no one to take lessons from. My father had always relied on my brother for support and decision making. My mother, I soon discovered, was like Ronald Reagan. She was capable of conveying emotion and holding the family together in public. In private her nerves were destroyed and she was not the leader I thought she was. Death undresses us all. It reveals our fears and secrets. My parents were both afraid of becoming sick and dying. Death was always visiting someone in Brooklyn. A distant relative you met at a Christmas or Easter dinner was dead. It didn't affect you because you hardly knew the person. But to lose one's brother at the age of forty-two, this was something that changed the world I lived in.

I closed the bathroom door in my parents' house. I look into the mirror at my face. I have been in New York for just two days getting things in order. I have aged. I can tell by the changes around my eyes. My face has changed the way the faces of presidents change after a crisis: Clinton, Carter, Kennedy. Give someone a Bay of Pigs or a hostage situation and one's face changes forever.

V

"You were always good with words," my mother tells me after Richard's funeral. I am surprised to hear this remark coming from her. How long have I been good with words? My mother sounds as if she is talking about a number runner. I'm the young guy good with figures running the streets of the neighborhood. But no . . . she has been moved by my eulogy of my brother. Words serving like an old blanket or quilt covering my head, healing me as I prepare to walk this road alone.

VI

In December 1986, my book party for *Where Are the Love Poems for Dictators?* was held in the Longworth Building on Capitol Hill. Mario Castillo, who was on the D.C. Arts Commission was also the chief of staff of the House Agricultural Committee. He helped to coordinate the affair. Photographer Harlee Little took pictures that evening and photographed my father, who had made only his third trip to Washington. In a few months I would be asking Harlee for a copy of the print to use for a funeral program.

Whenever a professional photographer is shooting in a room filled with people, he will often frame a shot, by asking folks to pose. While getting ready to snap the flash, someone with one of those instamatic cameras will jump in to take a picture as if it were a jam session and their horn was hot. In this instance, I think it was my cousin Kenny who gave someone his camera to take a picture of our family. The person missing in the photograph was my brother Richard. He has resurrected himself inside my memory. I push myself further into words.

CHAPTER SIXTEEN

I

During the first year after my brother's death I felt "protected" by his spirit. I knew good things would begin to happen in my life and career. One day a letter came in the mail from the Iraqi government, inviting me to the Al-Mirbad Poetry Festival in Baghdad. A paid trip to the Middle East. Al-Mirbad takes its name from an old marketplace in Basra where Arab poets once gathered. The opportunity to travel is important for most artists. It offers a chance to step outside of one's culture, to cross the border into new territory, and to network. I knew the Iraqi government was trying to develop a better world image and improve its relationship with the United States. I was not naive. Whenever I traveled abroad I tried to be aware of the image I was projecting as I promoted African American culture. I see all trips as a way to counter the negative stereotypes that too many people in the world have of African Americans. It's important that as black people we claim the international arena. I often view myself as a cultural ambassador. I talk about poetry, sports, politics, and race relations.

The trip to Iraq was not without risks. Iran and Iraq

had been launching missiles back and forth. While in Baghdad, two missiles exploded near the hotel where I was staying. One fell in a crowded residential area killing fifty-three people. Being in a war zone makes you think about life more. Attending the poetry festival and sightseeing and going to places like Babylon was something I was certain would never again happen in my life. I was a member of a small American delegation of poets, which included Gregory Orfalea and Michael Waters. We read a few poems, and spoke to a lot of people. I was surprised to see a large number of Sudanese workers walking around sections of Baghdad as if it were Harlem.

Outside my hotel window I could see the Euphrates River. I thought of Langston Hughes and his famous poem "The Negro Speaks of Rivers," which he dedicated to W. E. B. DuBois. Here I was on the other side of the world, the trip made possible because of my writing. I seldom write poems while on the road. I try to digest as much as possible. An image might return years later. I was happy to visit some of the mosques while in Iraq. It was strange to travel to Babylon and watch the rebuilding taking place. So often I had heard or read references to this place. Well, there I was a stranger in Babylon. I took pictures with my small camera.

I thought a lot about Richard while in Iraq. Here was a place he would have loved to visit. My brother was also on my mind because Denise was pregnant again. I had learned this a few months before the trip. A second child, a baby coming not long after my brother's departure. What folktale might mention how a spirit could return? Denise and I knew this second child was going to be a boy. How difficult to raise a manchild in this promised land. Fatherhood, for me now, was about doing things again. More diapers and waking in the middle of the night. Was I ready?

Denise and I prepared ourselves for another change in our lives. Did this spirit have a name?

II

I met my brother at Kennedy Airport the night he left for Iraq. I insisted on seeing him off. Since Richard's death I realized I needed to connect with my baby brother. I never knew he was doing so many things and knew so many people. I told him to bring me back a necklace or a rug. I would love to have something from that part of the world. I really started collecting things and fixing up my apartment. The entire place is white. I don't want to see any dirt anywhere. Family is important to me. What do I need to feel complete? Weeks before Richard died I had refused to talk to him. He was always complaining about something. I had heard it all before. Why can't people just start all over again if things don't work out? Look at Gene, a second wife and children. Traveling around the world. That's what I tell my parents they need to do. Get out and see things. You only live so long. "Your father doesn't want to go anywhere," my mother always says. "I'm stuck here," she complains. How does a woman get stuck if she's not even doing the driving? Sometimes I look at my mother and I feel she never lived for herself. The sad thing is that she prevents others around her from living their lives. Look at Richard. My brother was trapped working in a stupid bank his entire life. The only thing he had was the weekend, a Sunday when he could play the organ in church. I'm not going to live like that. My marriage was my last cage. Give me a ticket and I would be taking off with Gene right now. Zoom—I would like to fly away from here too.

III

Black boy. Black boy coming into the world. Denise is sitting in the hospital holding our son. She quietly asks me to come hold him. I take the small body and press it gently against my chest. Denise suddenly falls back in the bed. I yell for the nurse. She rushes in to help. She is followed by other staff members. I am told to leave the room. Black boy taken from my hands.

Denise is losing blood, pressure falling, life threatened. How many times have I heard a black mother say to her son, "Boy, do you know you almost killed me?" Not even a day old and my son's birth has made his presence known within his family. Things will never be the same. A black boy starting to make his way in this world.

So what do we call him? Nyere-Gibran. When I attended the Sixth Pan-African Congress in Tanzania in 1974, I had the opportunity to meet Julius Nyerere the president of Tanzania. What a gentle soul he was. Can a man govern an entire nation with warmth? I take his name and shorten it. I combine it with Gibran, the Lebanese poet, a writer whose work my brother loved. There was a time when he owned every book Gibran had written. Richard had found a used bookstore in Greenwich Village that had a large collection of Gibran's work. We later purchased a recording of his work being recited by a popular radio disc jockey. I wanted to connect my son to names whose

140

greater significance he could later discover. I hoped the name Nyere would make my son more aware of Africa and Gibran would remind him to always have poetry in his life.

Black boys with names that seem to fit like large sweaters. How sad to read the newspapers and see black boys being arrested with names like Kwame and Sekou, being captured as if it were slavery all over again. Black boys in jails like ships, packed. Bed to bed and cell to cell. Another long voyage to slavery? Police catching and taking away black boys like slave traders. Give them names to hold when everything else is taken. Hold a name in your mouth. Taste it. Speak your name and let the word free you. Nyere-Gibran, one day old, and knocking even his own mother down.

IV

Around midnight and I feel the quietness of the apartment. No noise on Fuller Street. Spring trying to grow through the urban air. April in Washington. Nyere is home. My friend and fellow writer Dan Moldea has helped me once again bringing my baby home. This time my mother is visiting from New York. She wants to help. Her hair gray, she has survived the death of one child and witnessed the birth of two grandchildren. She is counting blessings and miracles. There is a distance between us now filled by small bodies. My mother talks to me only about the children. Once it was Richard and Marie. Now it's Jasmine and Nyere. It's late at night and I have the front room to myself, and no space is too big to write a poem or two. I need to find something that is my own. The poems return even from my dark side.

V

How old is a young writer? I had goals and dreams to accomplish by the time I was thirty-five. Now I face the twilight of my thirties and then I turn forty. From 1974 until the 1980s began to slow down, I had sponsored poetry readings for an entire generation of new writers. They came through the *Ascension* readings and took their careers into the high realms of African American culture. If one was starting an expansion baseball league, maybe the type of new clubs critics like Harold Bloom would prefer us to play in, then here are my *Ascension* picks before the 1990s. These writers touched my life and maybe in some small way I helped to open a door (or window) for them: Stephanie Stokes, Donna Mungen, Michelle Parkerson, Winston Napier, Essex Hemphill, Sheila Crider, Jonetta Barras, Thulani Davis, Greg Tate, Joy Jones, Maghan Keita, Michael Harris, Calvin Reid, Marquette Folley, Gloria Hull, Dolores Kendrick, Michael Weaver, Peter Harris, A. L. Nielsen, Kimiko Hahn, Sharyn Skeeter, Garth Tate, Ken Forde, Reuben Jackson, and Monifa Love.

Almost every week I meet a new writer. Some need help, a few therapy, others a gentle push and encouragement. I've seen dreams realized because of determination and hard work. Terry McMillan comes quickly to mind. I remember talking with her on the phone before the publication of *Mama*. Here was a talented sister getting little help from folks in the literary community. How many other writers out there like her? Everyone wants to make it but what do they want to make? A best-seller? An appearance on the *Oprah* show? If one's career is a destination instead of a journey it will eventually end in disappointment. It's a cliché that always deserves repeating.

VI

The blues sets in after the romance. When loves fades it turns blue. The blues is sadness opening it's eyes early the next morning and asking how last night was. My father seldom argued with my mother. He did talk to himself, holding conversations in the next room as if he was a college professor delivering a lecture to a group of students who only want to know what was going to be on the final exam. With two children, there were moments when I saw myself becoming my father. I might be sitting at the dinner table, eating my food, lifting a fork slowly to my mouth, my head held up by my hand. Suddenly the realization that this is it. Your life is not going any further. Everything from this moment on is ritual: birthdays, Father's Day, Christmas . . .

By the end of the 1980s Denise and I had so much space between us we could have called it Iowa. We were one of those couples with children in the backseat and problems in the front. She had recommended so many self-help books that I could have built a front porch for my depression. What was wrong?

I think it started when my father walked over to my mother at the Savoy and asked her to dance. What if it was the song he loved more than the woman? Was it just his destiny? Karma? A person turns a corner and their life changes. A man wakes up next to his wife and decides to leave. Why? What music does he hear? Are we still haunted by the blues and train whistles? "I could have left your mother," my father told me one night when I was young and still afraid of the dark. Was he trying to convince himself to stay? February 1987, the start of another Black History Month. My father leaves my mother a widow. This is just a reminder I conclude, another black fact I must not forget.

VII

Very few members of my family have ever read my poetry. It's more important to them that I work at Howard University and live in Washington. In conversations I might as well be in the West Indies. There is always a promise to visit. My name is mentioned in much the same way people talk about food and the menu in a restaurant. At my father's funeral I gave the eulogy. Richard had gone ahead to open the door. I tried to find the words that would help to summarize my father's life. Fathering words, placing love on a black man's grave.

CHAPTER SEVENTEEN

I

I am almost fifty years old. The last few years I've been in love with a man who was much older then me. He is a beautiful doctor from Haiti. I didn't know what my parents would think. They can be quiet when they don't approve of someone. They can be listening to you while they are eating and never digest a word coming out of your mouth. I think my mother hated for me to be so happy. It reminded her of what was missing in her life. It meant that she would wake up in the morning and the phone would no longer ring. Forgotten. Ignored. Not me. I wanted to be treated like a queen. I wanted the good things in life. I wanted the things that were missing from my marriage. I can't accept a life spent simply cooking and cleaning for a man. I want to travel and sit in front of fireplaces while the snow is falling. I want to feel the ocean and sun on my face as I close my eyes while sailing on one of those cruises to the Caribbean. I don't want to die poor and unhappy. I want the good times even without the good man.

The day after my father died. I held my mother's head against my chest. We were in the bedroom and she was crying. I saw how small she was. When did this happen? The bedroom also small, and now empty. My father's clothes still hanging over a chair. On the dresser the pictures of me and Richard, and many pictures of Jasmine. Baby pictures capturing those moments when we were unaware of looking into the camera. In these pictures we don't even worry about posing because we are so happy and the world knows we are alive. "Marie," my lover whispers again and again, "you make me feel young again." It's true, I have this power over men. I hold my mother in my arms and feel her weakness. The spell she cast over our family is finally broken. She no longer needs to control another person's life.

II

Forty-two. Richard's age when he died in his sleep. Just the thought that my life could be over motivates me to work, to push myself. I start pulling together a large collection of poems. How much have I written? I have notebooks filled with much of my early work. Poems I wrote while living in Cook Hall. There are poems written to friends that I never published, and of course all the personal stuff that needs a good rewriting.

Finding a good publisher for poetry is always difficult. If you don't know anyone in the publishing business, then you're going to have problems. It's good to attend book fairs and conferences to get to know editors. Washington benefited from a person like Ahmos Zu-Bolton. Editors and publishers like Rick Peabody and Karren Alenier make a big difference in any literary community.

As a black poet my options were limited. I had to look beyond Lotus Press and even Haki Madhubuti's Third World Press in Chicago. These companies were being bombarded with manuscripts. Too many people trying to get in the door. It was like standing on line in Union Station during the Thanksgiving holiday, trying to catch an Amtrak train to New York. Someone in front of you has a ton of luggage and the line isn't moving. One person who produces beautiful books is Paul Coates of Black Classic Press in Baltimore. I had first met him when he sold books in front of Cramton Auditiorium at Howard. Paul had been a member of the Black Panther Party and then decided to open a black bookstore in Baltimore. We knew each other the way a person learns to acknowledge someone in the Nation of Islam. In other words, we spoke or nodded when we saw each other. Paul's love for books would lead him into library science and eventually a job with the Moorland-Spingarn Research Center at Howard University; located downstairs from where I worked. He soon discovered there were important black documents and books that were out of print, black classics waiting for someone to resurrect and introduce to a new generation of readers. Paul loved history and would become excited over the work of even the most obscure black historian. When it came to poetry, Paul would often laugh and say something like, "Bert, I don't know." Black Classic Press had published only one other poet and that was Liani Mataka. She had been one of those writers whose career took off after reading on a Baltimore radio station. Late at night and you're in someone's car caught at a red light listening to poetry on the air. Liani would be putting those words out into the dark for blues people and midnight lovers. For Paul to live in Baltimore, publish books, and not print her work would be like telling a rookie during spring training that Cal Ripken was going to miss a game. Not this year.

I think it was friendship that made Paul consider doing one of my books of poetry. I also felt my career had reached a point where it was a good investment for him. Being an active poet and writer, giving readings, maintaining a high public profile, I felt it would not be difficult to sell books. If a poet does not have an active career, the book will place a burden on a publisher. Reviews are not going to sell a lot of poetry books. It's word of mouth and hearing a poet at a reading or in a school that moves a title from the bookshelf to the checkout counter. Poetry can sell if one understands the business of poetry.

My goal was to share what I knew with Paul. I started working on a book that would pull together much of what I was proud to have written. I had reached the same age as my brother had been the year he died. This was a reminder, an encouragement to try and accomplish something each day. Richard's death had been unpredictable; so could mine. I was also moving into that territory, beyond the frontier, where people watch the role of the dice. Heart problems, cancer, AIDS, you name it. Or maybe you turn a corner and some young punk points a gun at your head. It's over and people are sending sympathy cards to your family. So I might as well get my stuff together. In the 1950s, folks were taking canned goods to their basement bomb shelters. Survival was what it was all about. I pulled poems from notebooks and files. I could be packing cans in a grocery store. I name the collection *First Light,* the title poem written after an overdose of Raymond Carver's work. It's a poem which simply attempts to cap-

148

ture the routines of daily life. One line makes reference to unfinished work on a desk. How different my life is from my father's. Work on a desk. Does this represents the movement away from manual labor? Is it a step into the middle class?

III

I have always been fascinated by individuals whose lives have been touched by God. Folks just like myself, walking around and then BOOM. The next thing you know they have a Bible open during lunchtime and want you to come to their church on Sunday. My father was always suspicious of people who talked too much about religion. I was primarily a reader when it came to things that were spiritual. Give me a good book about Islam or Buddhism and I think I can find my own way. Still, there are those moments when printed material is not enough. The soul is hungry for salvation and revelations. In 1993, I had an opportunity to leave Washington and take a teaching position in Nevada. It was a flight to the desert and it came at the right time. Both my father and brother had been stuck in the same job their entire life. The post office, a bank, a pension, and retirement. It was what my mother called a good job.

The idea of leaving Howard and going somewhere else was not something I went to bed thinking about. I had made a commitment to working at a black institution and nothing except death was going to change my mind. Live black, stay black, and die black. It was the type of decision that went beyond wearing an afro and reading black books. I was trying to make a difference with my life. Many student activists, writers, and scholars came through the African American Resource Center at Howard. It was a chance to share ideas and opinions. It was a great job. So when novelist and friend Richard Wiley called from the University of Nevada at Las Vegas (UNLV) inquiring about names to fill a position teaching African American literature, I provided him with a list of names that included such writers as Amiri Baraka and David Nicholson. I knew working in Las Vegas was not going to appeal to everyone, but it was a job at a time when many folks needed something. Trying to find work for folks was something I was doing. Writing letters of recommendation, forwarding job announcements, passing on telephone numbers, you name it, I was doing it. When Wiley called a second time and asked if I would be interested in the job, I said yes, without even thinking. I was certain my name was just being added to complete a list.

IV

Every man has the wilderness, the desert inside him, an open place filled with trees and sometimes with nothing. It's a combination of one's past and future. How many of us keep searching, restless as the ocean, moving in and out of jobs and relationships? I was reaching a point in my life where I needed to know if I had made the right decision to become a writer. I was also holding onto the hat of father and husband. One part of me was fighting domestic routines, the sharing of space with others. Wife, daughter, and son meant responsibilities. Another part of me still wanted to fly. Was this the poet, always waiting to fall in love again and again?

There were a couple of female roommates between my

marriages. These relationships I guess left me with sexual scars and emotional tissue torn inside the heart. Maybe I wasn't ready to settle down. Or was it because I now saw my father's coat hanging in my own closet? His shoes, polished and waiting for me to try on? Was I walking into my father's life? A quiet rage began to spill over into my poems. I became very moody around Denise. I saw her responding to me in much the same manner as my mother had to my father.

When UNLV agreed to hire me it was almost as if I had begun to plot my escape from Washington, Denise, Howard, and everything else I couldn't face. I felt as if I was Crystal at the end of Ntozake Shange's *For Colored Girls,* talking about having no air. It was time for me to go to Nevada. Even Denise thought the change and distance might be good for whatever I was going through. She kept waiting for me to talk about what was bothering me. What could I say? Where were my words? I was in my early forties, writing poems, still publishing in little magazines and small presses. I was hosting readings and radio programs. Was this going to be the best I could hope to achieve?

Coming from Iowa, I knew my wife missed having a home and a backyard. We were a family of four in a two-bedroom apartment in Adams Morgan. It could have been Longwood Avenue in the Bronx. I left Washington in January 1993 and went to Las Vegas. It was a gamble. I was juggling. But I could feel my brother's spirit helping to shuffle the cards. That cold January morning was like him opening a window back in the old neighborhood. Why was I suddenly thinking about Richard again? Why did the desert in Nevada seem so attractive? Why did I feel I was defeating a similar demon to the one that had knocked my father down? Richard and Egberto, two black men whose

151

dreams fell out of their pockets before they even knew there were holes in their coats.

V

Chris Hudgins, the chairman of the English Department, showed me where my office was. I was excited about my first teaching job. I felt as if I had been traded to another league. From Howard to UNLV. From the East to the West. I had a nice two-bedroom apartment about one block away from the campus. Everything I needed was in walking distance.

VI

The weekends are the difficult days. I knew I would miss my children. I'd miss those January Sundays, filled with NFL playoffs and then the Super Bowl followed by the NBA games, when I was happy to be home and not feeling guilty about not being at the Smithsonian looking at art that's supposed to be good for me. We shared the chips, the dip, the cookies, and the game was the center of our attention, and it's better being with my son and daughter and not the guys from work because these are the moments my children will describe to their families long after I'm gone. The telephone would ring, and Nyere and Jasmine would look at me. They knew to tell the caller that I'm not home. This time it's true. I'm in Las Vegas living alone.

I keep waiting for something to happen. This is Vegas, a place where things revolve around luck and gambling. I am fortunate to be working on *In Search of Color Everywhere*. It's a project literary agent Marie Brown was able to secure for me. Lena Tabori of Stewart, Tabori & Chang (STC) wanted to publish an anthology of African American poetry. It was to be a coffee table book, something with a handsome design. When the project was just an idea, I started thinking about how great it would be to have all the well-known African American poems in one volume. The design of the book would make it a classic. I was familiar with books done by STC; they often won awards for book design.

In order to make the anthology unique, I had to develop a fresh way of presenting the poetry. I decided on a thematic framework and arrangement. The idea of themes or sections, was more appealing than listing contributors in alphabetical or chronological order. When Quincy Troupe and Rainer Schulte edited *Giant Talk* in 1975, it immediately became one of my favorite books. I liked the idea of looking at literature in its political context and classifying things under such headings as "Oppression and Protest," "Music, Language, Rhythm," and "Ritual Magic." I decided to structure my anthology using categories that I felt African American literature could easily be placed within. Stephen Henderson taught me that the major theme running throughout African American literature was the theme of freedom and liberation. Following this, one would find a large body of work wrestling with the problems of identity and blackness.

With, *In Search of Color Everywhere*, I wanted to create the type of book that should have been in my house back in the Bronx. Here was the book I wanted Ms. Greenfield and Ms. Fontana, my elementary teachers, to open and read. While other children hid under their desks fearing the dropping of a nuclear bomb, I could have been listening to the words of Dunbar, Hughes, and Cullen. I could have been a fourth or fifth grader thinking about Africa. I might have wanted to be a blues or jazz musician and take one of my mother's berets from her closet. If I had just one poetry book, filled with the cream and sugar of tradition, I could have tasted pride and placed a few more pounds on my bones. Nothing worse than being skinny and feeling miserable and ignorant.

VII

I can't believe my brother took a job in Nevada. Why? He's on the other side of the moon and it's just me here taking care of Enid. Sometimes it's just too much. I can't drive everyday from Yonkers to the end of Manhattan. I have a life, or maybe I want one. It's me who places flowers on the graves of my brother and father. Everyone else is always too busy. Between the hospital and keeping my house clean and maybe going to see a movie or a friend, how much time do I have left for myself?

When I was a young girl, the magazines I read told me how to become a woman. They said I needed a man to be happy. If I could fix my hair, my nails, my teeth, my skin, then I could attract a man and maybe even love. Now I'm old enough to realize that those ads were lies and just a way to get you to subscribe to desire for another year.

I started reading and collecting black books. I love to read mysteries because they appear to be so much like what I live. My family has always been a mystery, especially the men. My father and brothers were always talking about what they were going to do in life or how life had given them a slice of bread with no butter. I thought I knew men, but then my husband and my lovers were mysteries too. I became a part of their stories, their tales. Do you know what it's like to be someone's story? You exist only for that person and your life has it's end, but you don't know it. The author doesn't share it with you. Nothing worse then having your voice trapped on the page. It's like losing your soul or color. You have to learn how to rise, open the door, and search for it everywhere.

CHAPTER EIGHTEEN

I

When was the first time I started keeping secrets? Or was it just silence? Things unspoken and never told. I sit outside my apartment in Las Vegas, looking at the lights shining over the Strip. The night air is still warm and there are a pile of books on my living room table. I've been reading all day, stopping only for a few moments to write a poem. Now, a gray cat meows and brushes against my leg. I always associate cats with my brother. He was a lover of animals but especially cats. He saw them as guardians of the soul. Whenever I see a cat appear out of nowhere, I take it as a good omen. Funny, how we search for meanings in things.

While in Las Vegas, I received a letter from an old friend, Barbara-lyn Morris. She sent me a copy of her family newsletter. I had met Barbara-lyn in the late seventies when I gave a talk at the World Future Society Conference held in Washington, D.C. Barbara-lyn and her family were living in Richmond at the time. She was working at a high school and invited me down to read some poems. Barbara-lyn's husband, Tom, was now president of Emory & Henry College in Emory, Virginia. An exchange of letters between

Las Vegas and Emory resulted in an invitation to visit the small college located in the hip pocket of Virginia near the Tennessee border. A reading and visit with Barbara-lyn and Tom opened the door to the possibility of being a visiting professor at Emory & Henry College.

How do you know who will influence your life? Suddenly, a cat walks across your path and you think about your luck or maybe that a spirit is watching over you. Chance, a toss of the dice and you gamble or maybe you finally realize what faith is. How do you begin to embrace the unseen?

II

On April 15, 1993, I delivered the UNLV 27th Honors Convocation address. My topic was "The Poet as Witness." James Baldwin wrote about the difference between the witness and the observer. The witness is moved by compassion and the need to give testimony. This is how I feel now. The months in Nevada have given me more confidence in myself. The completion of book projects has opened new doors. I am ready.

Denise and my children came out to Las Vegas for my speech. The trip served as a birthday gift for both Nyere and Jasmine. We are a family that travels a lot but seldom together. Some principle of synergy works at the dinner table. At times marriage can be like that double consciousness DuBois talked about: a battle taking place for your soul and you try to keep from being torn apart.

It was strange to have my family living in my Las Vegas apartment, even for a few days. How quickly one becomes use to solitude, space, and quiet. Could I live this way forever?

III

For a brief moment I think about staying in Las Vegas.
Like a Cuban baseball player or boxer waiting for the next
Olympics. See you later, Fidel. I could slip into Miami or
somewhere and start over or maybe simply dream. Poetry
has been very good to me. Richard Wiley tells me to think
it over. I stare at Sunrise Mountain in the distance. Langston Hughes once lived in Reno and maybe only missed
Harlem when someone hummed something by Ellington.
Wallace Thurman was born in Salt Lake City, so this frontier has known colored writers before.

If I were a fiction writer with a reputation, I would
seriously consider staying. I completed *In Search of Color
Everywhere* while at UNLV, an impossible task if I had
stayed at Howard, working without a fax machine or computer. I have a number of students like Tom and Tracie
Guzzio that make this journey a wonderful experience.
They are both serious about black studies and are not held
back by their lack of pigmentation. I like the look of this
place. The redness. The flatness. The heat. The only problem is the isolation from cultural and political events
around the country. The time zones can keep one in the
past. When I talk to people back East, I feel as if they are
part of the Harlem Renaissance while I'm sharecropping
down South or looking for gold out West.

IV

What are the colors of poems? Mine began to change in
Las Vegas. I started writing about my family. My mother
appears in much of my work. The image is not of a Ma-
donna but instead, a working-class woman, wrestling with

159

the past and fearful of the future. How often did I hear my mother praying for strength and asking for God's blessing? The mother, so all consuming. Where are the words for my father? What simple images are now so precious to my memory. My father reaching into his closet for a hat. His brown hands trying to show mine how to tie a tie. I write poems trying to bring back the Bronx. My father looking at his face in the mirror, afraid of growing old; washing his hands in the bathroom sink with Ivory soap. What did these rituals mean? Who will unlock my poems and discover the meaning of fatherhood?

It is the distance between fathers and sons that shape so many of our lives. We are separated by oceans, cities, jobs, wars, divorce, and death. I talk with Nyere on the telephone. I too have failed to send him letters. Why do we find it difficult to write or talk with our boys? I could be a letter misplaced by my father's hands, one of the few mistakes he made while working in the post office. Here I am in Nevada, miles away from my son, my daughter, Jasmine, perhaps thinking that this is how it begins. A black man says he loves you and then disappears. Does it begin with one's father? Sons and daughters looking at their fathers and measuring the distance between love and pain. I try to convince myself that I am working to provide for them, but then there are those places inside of me that understand the need to be alone.

Is this what my brother discovered hidden in the work of Thomas Merton? The inner voice struggles to close its ears to the sounds of the world, and a thing called desire. I rise and look out my window at Sunrise Mountain. Morning prayers burning slowly like incense and days slipping away. Breathe, I tell myself, catch your breath and breathe.

V

I work during vacations. I need to get away from the hospital. I need to get away from my mother. I need to have a life of my own. It isn't fair to look into a mirror and realize my life is almost over. Who wrote this story?

VI

Many of my friends didn't know I was living and working in Nevada until I was back in Washington walking along Columbia Road. Many of my relationships exist on paper or can be reduced to short telephone conversations. Change the return address on an envelope and no one will even notice—I'm gone. But I did. I felt better. I had changed my job, something my father would never had done. He was a man who had never taken risks. He was comfortable knowing a regular paycheck was coming in. The forties and fifties and my father knew best.

Returning to Howard was difficult. At UNLV I had worked one day a week, my salary much higher. I now had experienced the academic world beyond the color line of Howard, Hampton, Morgan, Morehouse, and Fisk. I was now Mookie, trying to do the right thing.

VII

It doesn't matter where you live, family relationships change over a period of time. I was becoming more aware of the importance of my sister in my life. One can suddenly look around and discover that your platoon has taken a few hits. Who is left? I counted an uncle in Baltimore, an aunt in New Jersey, a faceless crowd of cousins who could have been winners in a lottery contest, and my mother and sister. My brother, when he was alive, always talked about how members of our family would emerge from woodwork to claim an inheritance once one of us became known beyond the borders of the housing projects.

This became obvious after the publication of *In Search of Color Everywhere*. The book was published in 1994 and immediately became popular with readers and collectors. Illustrator Terrance Cummings was primarily responsible for providing attractive artwork, which simply enhanced the work in the collection. I was pleased with creating what I felt was a black classic, something that would last beyond book tours, talk shows, and reviews. At the first book party, held at Rizzoli in New York, not far from the office of Stewart, Tabori & Chang, I got a taste of how things were changing. In the middle of a sea of writers and friends, a very tall, beautiful woman appeared. She had that Ellington Cotton Club look, or maybe it was Lena Horne all over again. No, Dorothy Dandridge waiting for the world to stop. Looking over the crowd and then into my eyes she inquired as to where Ethelbert Miller was. "Who are you?" I asked. I felt like a detective who was interviewing a suspect at the beginning of a movie. "I'm his cousin," the tall woman responded. Well, kick me down a flight of stairs and then put a sign on my back that says, "Kick me again." Who was this woman? Only my mother could tell me later the next day when I called her from a hotel room in Boston. "Oh, that was one of your cousins, on your father's side," she said. "Who?" was my only response. Sometimes when I am traveling, I call my mother. She likes to receive tele-

162

phone calls and postcards. I talk to her and it feels like I'm ordering room service. Our conversations are just long enough for me to inquire about dessert.

VIII

I don't have much to do with many of them. Family? Please. Family is my mother, Gene, Aunt Evelyn, and cousins Kenny and Cliff. Family is my father's brother in Baltimore. I don't know the rest. When I go to a funeral, I only recognize the person in the box.

I am happy that my baby brother is doing well. I was so tickled when I saw his book *In Search of Color Everywhere*. I showed a copy to everyone at work. I told doctors at the hospital about the book. I let them know those words were as good as medicine.

IX

Black romance. The books are everywhere. What's love got to do with it? When I started writing, love was the central theme of my work. I included some of my old love poems in *First Light*. I went back and pulled things I had written when I was in college. Poems to Michelle and other women who had changed my life. The work was now snakeskin. Around 1994, I started writing personal essays. I needed to dig deeper into myself. The spirit of my father began to visit me. Being a father after losing one is like slipping on ice and catching yourself. I was coming home to an apartment on Fuller Street in northwest Washington after a day at Howard. I could have been Egberto stepping in front of

163

a car on Longwood Avenue in the Bronx. Headlights coming at me as I jump to the curb and count my blessings.

One of my essays was published in *Picturing Us: African American Identity in Photography*, edited by Deborah Willis. The title was "In My Father's House There Were No Images." *Fathering Words* has its beginning in this anthology. Along with the essay there is a picture of my brother taken the day he left to go to the monastery. He is wearing a suit and tie. Two bags are next to his feet. My brother is smiling. It's a picture of letting go and spiritual satisfaction. There is no clue that he is saying good-bye to his family. I have no idea who took the picture. Was it my father? At night the men of my family comfort me. Their memories are now mine. I am a different type of picture. This is not a photograph but my life.

CHAPTER NINETEEN

I

$\mathcal{M}$y brother and I are discussing AIDS. Every now and then we have one of these talks. They take place when he comes to New York for a reading or meeting. I usually drive down from Yonkers to our mother's house in Tribeca. Parking is often difficult in the area. I remember when our parents first moved into their apartment, which has a wonderful view of the Hudson River and the New Jersey shore. The boats would pass and my father would stand on the terrace and look out at the water. I liked to sneak up behind him and place my arms around his shoulders. "Marie," he would say, guessing my name as if I were a cloud or some thought he had just pulled from the sky.

I started thinking about death when my parents moved from the Bronx. They came to the end of Manhattan to live what I knew were the last years of their lives. Their apartment was not home to me. When Gene came up from Washington, he slept on the sofa in the living room. It was the same couch we all had sat in when we were younger. It had been a wedding gift belonging to our parents. It was good furniture, the kind you couldn't find anymore. When we were children we were reminded never to place our feet on the upholstery. It was bad manners and against the religion of West Indian upbringing or maybe it was just a folktale to remind you never to sit with your hands behind your head or your father might die.

My brother and I talk and laugh. We are loud and our conversation worries our mother who tries to tell us to hush, to lower our voices. "People can hear every word you're saying," she says. Gene laughs and we talk some more. We talk about what's going on at the hospital and in the world. It's moments like this when I look around at the three of us and think about the family not being smaller but just closer. Even when my mother talks to herself or falls asleep, then it's my brother and I sharing food and maybe a cold beer. So who cares if the Knicks lost again and Gene is a Bulls fan. The season never ends on our love. I look at the pictures my mother has on the piano and the ones next to the lamp and on top of the television. They are photographs of Jasmine and Nyere. The grand-children's smiles are what keeps my mother warm when she turns off the kitchen light and heads into the bedroom to hug the other pillow on the bed. Some nights when I am driving back to Yonkers, I look over at the Hudson on my left and see the lights flickering. "Marie," I whisper to myself. The sound of my name is all I hear.

II

There are a number of African American male writers who have discovered their own voices within their father's houses. I think of John Wideman, Alexs Pate, and Cornelius Eady, all trying to fix words on paper. Their books are important to me. I started reading Eady's poetry at my own readings. This permitted me to step outside myself to connect my own work with that of another poet. Eady's work was difficult to write. The pain and ridicule he suffered from his father were the key ingredients necessary to write *You Don't Miss Your Water*. My relationship with my father was different. I was searching for something that would connect me with him now that he is dead. My father was someone I didn't have the chance to know. My brother benefited from being first, for catching my father when he was young and walking around with a camera taking pictures of his new family. Coming through the late sixties and early seventies, I was fascinated by the black activist Ron Karenga's emphasis on the need to create a mythology. This was what I wanted to do as I struggled to write about my father. Was he not a myth?

Like Camilo and Che who were with Fidel in the mountains, I wait for my beard to grow, my facial hair marking my arrival and place in the scheme of things. Why do I believe this? Both my father and brother were men who grew such wonderful beards during the years just before their deaths. It's a form of measurement of my life against theirs. Nothing matters as much as writing this memoir. It is almost a prayer. A prayer for Egberto and Richard. Two men who were left with only their faith. Two men with a sadness so blue it could be black. Two men who placed their hearts inside my mother's hands only to feel her squeeze the happiness out. Responsibility I keep calling it. Be responsible like my father and brother.

III

The poet Pinkie Gordon Lane calls my office one day in 1995. How can I recall the exact date? So many things forgotten, even this book consists of only fragments glued together. This is memory. My biography can be found in the many files I've collected over the years. They wait for a scholar or graduate student hungry for a reputation. My files are like unedited tapes, something Nixon would understand. My letters, diaries, and interviews are all being cataloged at Emory & Henry College in Emory, Virginia. How they got there is linked to Pinkie's call. She had been a Jessie Ball duPont visiting scholar at a college in Virginia. She told me about a program that placed writers and scholars on the campuses of many of the schools located in Virginia. When I received additional information from Pinkie I saw that Emory & Henry College was one of the participating institutions. I had received an invitation from Barbara-lyn and Tom Morris to work at Emory & Henry when I was in Nevada. Now I had the opportunity.

IV

*W*hen my mother called and told me that Ethelbert was receiving an honorary doctorate from a school in Virginia, I just knew I had to find something special to wear. I knew I had to be there. I made plane reservations for the two of us. No way I was driving. I

168

don't even go to Brooklyn. Traveling with my mother is always an adventure. She worries about everything and then sometimes she just goes off to sleep and I think about how tired her eyes are. A woman needs to close her eyes sometimes, not to sleep but to rest. When we reach seventy or eighty we can do what we want. We can stand, sit, or even fly. Enid is flying and her life is up here in the clouds next to mine.

Emory is different from New York. I meet so many people I can't keep the names straight. Everyone is talking about my baby brother and I'm so proud to be his big sister, and maybe I don't have children but this is close enough. Enid, Denise, and I are sitting at the graduation ceremony. Someone asks us to stand and we do. I hear the applause wash over my mother's head. She is wearing the hat I gave her. It keeps the sun out of her eyes. I know she is too proud to cry right now. Maybe she is thinking about my father and how he should be here. My mother is humming to herself, moving her head in a church-nodding fashion. "Amen," she whispers and there is something final about how she says this word. Like Jesus on the cross realizing it's time. If folks want a miracle from my mother, then this is it. I listen to my brother's commencement address and his words baptize me in the name of the father, the son . . .

V

There are many degrees and levels in life. Too often people change when they complete a level of learning. Malcolm X once mentioned that the black community had too many doctors and not enough cures. With each success and achievement that comes my way, I try to maintain a sense of humility. It's too easy for a writer to become self-centered. One best-selling book and a person refuses to stay at a Best Western hotel when touring. What is that about? If we remember that our art is a gift, then it's possible to keep things in perspective. Difficult but not impossible.

Being a father to Jasmine and Nyere was a challenge in the 1990s. Denise and I had created a small home on Fuller Street. We were quickly outgrowing the space as our children grew older. Being from Iowa, Denise was the type of woman who needed the backyard and front porch. Our children skipping into adolescence meant they needed space for birthday parties and sleepovers. I was living that quiet life of desperation and wanted a place for my books and papers. I was trapped, however, by how I had been raised. I was from a line of renters. Home ownership was like attempting to write a novel. What would I do if I had electrical or plumbing problems? Richard had lived in a Manhattan apartment near Riverside Drive. Marie was in Yonkers also looking at the Hudson. I had that funny feeling that I too would soon find a place next to a body of water. Maybe a house facing the ocean?

What was wrong with me? Hadn't I read all those black intellectual texts that mentioned the importance of land? Deep inside I knew that my inability to drive a car could be linked to my lack of household repair skills. What would happen if something went wrong? Did I want to come home after a poetry reading and cut grass or rake leaves? My father never owned much. His philosophy was built on the belief that one couldn't take anything with you when death came knocking. Yet I was always coming back from the homes of writers who were living well. Writer friends who had agents and contracts. Folks with book deals. I often felt like Bigger Thomas, watching airplanes in the sky. How many other Biggers are out there? The literary world is still segregated and reflective of how we live our lives.

I left the searching for a house to Denise. Actually, Denise decided she would plot a Tubmanlike escape and a journey to personal freedom. She had never been comfortable living in the Adams Morgan neighborhood of Washington. She found the area to be congested, her own pocket of air vandalized like a car left on a side street. In many ways our marriage became the mirror of what was wrong with the city. Our love was becoming a manuscript in need of an editor. Too often Denise reminded me of my mother. I was caught by surprise when she embraced the study of religion. Her pursuit of a divinity degree from Howard University was not what I expected her to do when we first met. Watching her study in the early morning hours brought back memories of Richard. The only thing missing were the candles. The only thing left to burn was myself.

CHAPTER TWENTY

I

So who am I? Could this be the opening chapter of Ellison's *Invisible Man?* I have at times taken refuge in the basement of my house on Underwood Street. In a room filled with boxes, filled with manuscripts, filled with the pages of my life and things held together by tape, paperclips, and rubberbands, there are items that have begun to peel, dry, and crumble. I sort through old poems like my father sorting the mail in the post office; scattering things to requested destinations. I read old love letters like Richard reading sacred texts. My life is not a long poem. It's more a document or legal text available for different interpretations. I started with what my father and brother gave me. The founding father and brother. My mother taught me to learn what was not in the text. Her wisdom can be traced through her years of marriage. My mother's love was that mysterious sound you heard in the house when you thought someone was breaking in.

II

I am waiting for Marie to arrive at Union Station. It is the first month of 1999. I invited her to Washington to see Nyere play basketball at the Edmund Burke School. She is traveling on the Amtrak from New York. My sister wanted a vacation. She has been taking care of Enid for the last several weeks. Age touches the temple of my mother, graying her hair. Now as Marie enters the terminal she appears not only to be my sister but she resembles my mother and all my aunts. I place my arm around her shoulder and the world turns into Coney Island and we are kids laughing on the Broadwalk looking for Nathan's. We are standing on the corner of Beck and Fox Streets in the Bronx. We are not in Union Station, but on Longwood Avenue staring at P.S. 39 on the big street. Marie is now Aunt Marie. The aunts are always the women who remind you of Bessie Smith and Ma Rainey. From hats to jewelry, they catch the world, and men can only shake their heads with admiration and step back. Aunts bring their own poems and stories when they come to visit or share your memoir.

III

*T*wo years ago it was Jasmine who came to visit. I had just moved into a larger apartment in Yonkers. God, the girl had grown overnight since the last time I saw her. Time flies, my mother always says, but then I guess it's age that spreads its wings across my face when I look into the mirror. We stayed up late that first night, laughing and talking about being a young lady. I showed her how to take care of her arms and legs. I had to show her how to fight the ash and restore the glow.

Jasmine was like the sister I never had. I wanted someone I could share secrets with, borrow sweaters from, talk about boyfriends and lipstick, maybe that first kiss or the way my hair was combed the day I did it myself. A sister is a sister, and a brother is the guy who becomes an uncle to your kids. But I never had children, so the space between me and my brothers grew over the years. I never really knew that until Richard died and my brother wrote *Fathering Words*.

IV

I wanted to be the father my father never was. I wanted to be like my father, the one he dreamed about being. When I was small he was big, when I was tall he was taller, when I saw him in the hospital fighting for his life, I was living on his air, his breath. It was something he gave me and could not take away. My father's love was measured by the distance between us. I became a writer because he lived a quiet life and my mother was afraid for us to speak, to draw attention to ourselves, to walk out into the world and perhaps cross a street or a sea as wide as memory. My father was the man I never knew, but the man I always saw. So quiet in his pain and suffering that I could not carry his cross, only his name, and even that I changed to fit myself. Sometimes I am just Ethelbert. No first or last name. No beginning or end. I am Ethelbert at sea, no connections, family or close friends. I can sit in airports and train stations with no desire to reach home. Fuller or Underwood it doesn't matter. I am fathering words, my own.

V

I am sitting next to Carmen in the funeral home. She looks into my eyes and says, "Your brother loved you." I think about the strangeness of her words. Did Richard first say these words when my mother was thinking about giving me to her mother's sister? When love is finally spoken, it changes the world. I wish I could learn to write it down. My friend June Jordan sends an E-mail that renovates my heart. It gives me the strength to believe in the future. She writes:

Dearest Ethelbert:

Tonight it's the first rain of the new year, the last year of the millennium.
And it is tonight that I sat at the table, reading your autobiographical excerpt.
Well, I am still breathing, and thank God for that!
You do bless my life
To go on loving means not to forget and you remember you testify and no one could doubt your love. And I do not forget your love, or mine—my love for you. I remember.
And the rain seems beautiful now. Clean and soft and everywhere just gentle and not to be denied.
Thank you. Adambert.
Thank you for what you have chosen to remember, and why.
You the Tallman, always.
The Tallman and The Loving Poet of my life.

June

CHAPTER TWENTY-ONE

I

It was my friend Don Mee Choi who watched me fall outside the Forty-fifth Street theater in Seattle in January
1999. I had slipped near a curb and fell backward into the
mud, hurting my elbow and ankle. Despite her immediate
concern with my well-being, Don Mee (a Buddhist) believed my fall was symbolic and necessary.

Perhaps I would not have written this book if I was not
still searching at this point in my life for what I call at
different times my bowl or bridge. In many ways I am still
a small boy watching my brother light candles on his home-
made altar. During the days before his departure to the
Trappist community of Our Lady of the Genesee in Piffard, New York, Richard would rise in the early morning
hours. Why did I never join him? Why did I not rise from
my bed? During our entire lives the closeness between us
was like a silent blackness. My brother never talked to me
about God or love when he returned from Piffard. It was
as if the poetry of his soul had been lost. He became very
much like my father. Lost. Yet, right before he died, Richard left a letter that he instructed a friend to give to me. It
was my mother who eventually handed me the envelope. I

had just arrived from Washington to help with Richard's funeral. "This is for you," my mother said, as she turned and walked back into the heat of the kitchen. I took the envelope and sat on the living room couch. It was the same couch that held my childhood in dark spaces under the cushions. The couch had survived almost fifty years of family lessons, and still I struggled to make sense out of who I was.

Richard's letter bore no stamp. Instead he had drawn two birds in pencil. Behind them were flowers. The birds on the envelope were ascending. Inside the envelope my brother had placed a folded black sheet of paper. No words, just a blank sheet of black paper.

Macon, Georgia
January 30, 1999